I0487312

A BEGINNER'S GUIDE TO
DATA SCIENCE

How to dive into the data ocean without drowning

ENAMUL HAQUE

All rights reserved. This book or any portion thereof may not be reproduced or used in any manner without the publisher's express written permission except for brief quotations in a book review or scholarly journal.

COPYRIGHT © 2021 ENAMUL HAQUE

All rights reserved
Enel Publications
London, UK

REVISION: 7

ISBN 978-1-4478-2655-2

Table of Contents

Limit of Liability/Disclaimer of Warranty

Information obtained from authentic and highly regarded sources is mentioned in the "Notes and References" section. Reprinted material is quoted, and sources are indicated. Reasonable efforts have been made to publish reliable data and information, but the author and publisher cannot assume responsibility for the validity of all materials or the consequences of their use. All information given in this book is based on the author's own research and does not constitute technical, financial, or professional advice.

Apart from the permissions received, the author and publisher have attempted to trace the copyright holders of all material reproduced in this publication and apologise to copyright holders if permission to publish in this form has not been obtained. If any copyrighted material has not been acknowledged, please write, and let us know so we may rectify it in future reprints.

Trademark Notice: Product or corporate names may be trademarks or registered trademarks and are used only for identification and explanation without intent to infringe. The author and publisher of this book are not liable or responsible for any other websites or services linked to or from it.

Introduction

Data science has become increasingly popular in recent years for several reasons.

First, the amount of data generated has grown exponentially due to the proliferation of digital technologies such as sensors, smartphones, and social media. This "big data" is being developed in various industries, including healthcare, finance, retail, and manufacturing. It can improve decision-making, increase efficiency, and drive innovation.

Second, technological advances have made collecting, storing, and analysing large amounts of data more accessible. Tools such as Hadoop and Spark, as well as cloud-based platforms like Amazon Web Services and Google Cloud, have made it easier for data scientists to work with large datasets.

Finally, data science has become increasingly important in gaining a competitive advantage. Companies and organisations using data effectively can better understand their customers, optimise their operations, and make better decisions. As a result, the demand for skilled data scientists has grown significantly, making it an in-demand and potentially lucrative career path.

Why it's science?

Like biological sciences, which investigate biology, and physical sciences, which examine how things work physically data science studies data. If we want to work with data, we need to understand its true qualities and that it is genuine.

When some academics reviewed the statistics curriculum in the 1980s and 1990s, they came up with a definition or nomenclature and decided that data science would be a better fit.

In fact, since ancient times, people have practised the skill of extracting insights and patterns from data. The ancient Egyptians used census information to boost the effectiveness of taxation and consistently anticipated the Nile river's annual flooding. Since that time, those who engage in data science have created a special and unique discipline for their work, which is called data science.

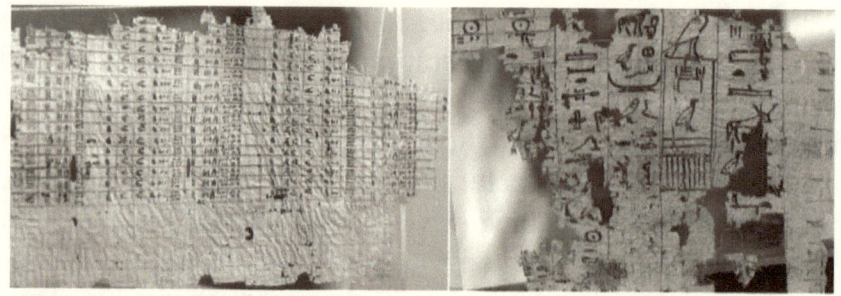

Figure 1 - Spreadsheets and checklists used by Egyptians for building pyramids

Data science is the practice of going through data analysis and trying to get some conclusions from it if you have data, are curious, and are working with, altering, and investigating it. It attempts to use data to discover solutions to topics being explored. In a sense, it has more to do with data than science.

Why it's so "HOT" now?

Data science is currently essential because there is an abundance of data available. There was a lack of data and no algorithms in the past, but now we have both. Additionally, software for data analysis is now open source and free, and it is also now possible to store and analyse large amounts of data at a low cost. The tools and resources for working with data are now easily accessible, making it an excellent time to be a data scientist.

The sexiest job

The phrase "sexiest job of the 21st century" is often used to refer to data science, as Harvard Business Review coined it in an article published in 2012. The paper argued that data science is the "sexiest" job because it involves technical skills (such as programming, statistics, and machine learning), business acumen, and the ability to communicate complex ideas effectively.

Data science has become increasingly important in recent years as the amount of data generated has grown exponentially. Companies and organisations in various industries use data science to make better decisions, improve efficiency, and gain a competitive advantage. As a result, the demand for skilled data scientists has grown significantly, making it an in-demand and potentially lucrative career path.

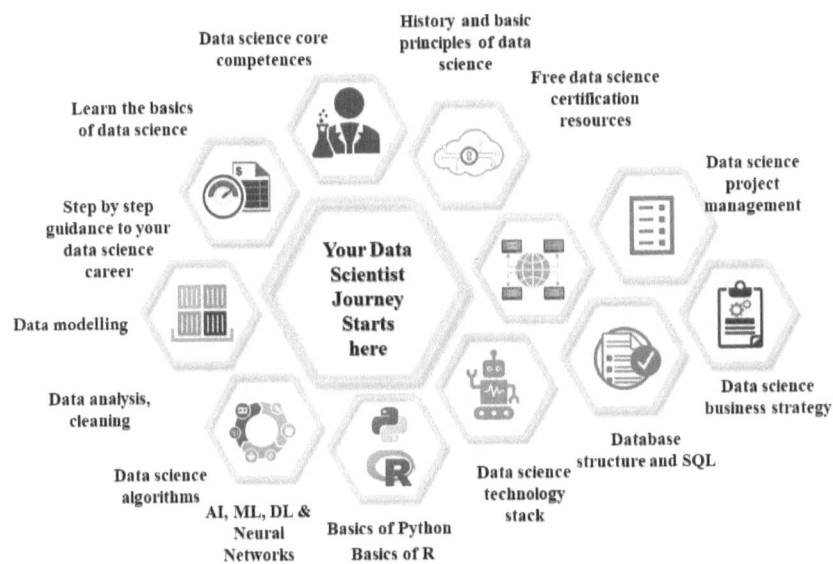

Figure 2 - Highlights of key features of this book

It's worth noting that the phrase "sexiest job of the 21st century" is a bit of a tongue-in-cheek way of describing the importance and attractiveness of data science as a career. It does not necessarily mean that data science is the most attractive or desirable job in the 21st century.

It is also the new oil

Data is often referred to as the "new oil" because, like oil, data is a valuable resource that can be extracted, refined, and used to generate value. Just as oil is used as a fuel to power vehicles and as a raw material for a wide range of products, data can be used to power businesses and inform decision-making.

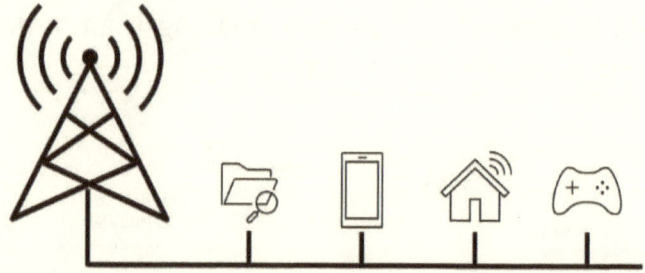

Figure 3 - Crude data could be extracted, refined, and used to generate value

Data has become increasingly important as a strategic asset for businesses and organisations. Companies are collecting and analysing large amounts of data to gain insights and make more informed decisions, and data is being used to drive innovation and improve operations.

Like oil, data is a finite resource that must be carefully managed and used efficiently. Data scientists and other professionals with data science skills are in high demand because they can extract value from data and use it to inform decision-making and drive innovation.

The notion that "data is the new oil" is related to how both commodities gain value in a similar manner. Similar to oil, raw data doesn't have value by itself; rather, value is produced when it is rapidly, completely, and properly obtained, as well as when it is related to other pertinent data. Also, the analogy of data being "the new oil" highlights the growing importance of data as a valuable resource and the need for professionals with the skills to extract insights and value from it.

Why learn data science?

Learning data science can help you gain valuable skills that can be applied in a wide range of career paths and can also help you better understand and make sense of the vast amounts of data that are generated and collected in the modern world.

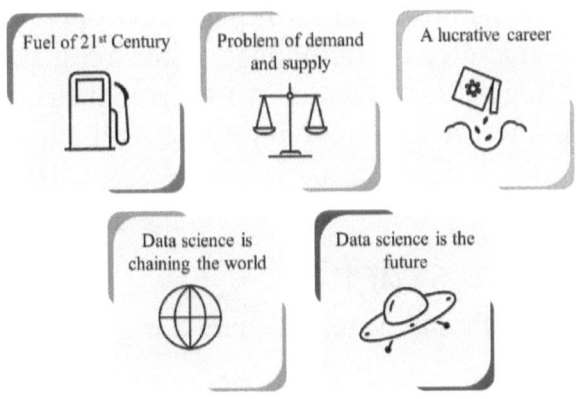

Figure 4 - Why learn data science?

Some specific reasons to learn data science include the following:

Demand for data scientists is high: There is a growing demand for professionals with data science skills, and this trend is expected to continue in the future. Data scientists are in high demand because they are able to extract insights and value from data, which is becoming increasingly important in today's data-driven world.

Data science skills are versatile: Data science skills can be applied in a wide range of industries and contexts, making them highly versatile and in demand.

Data science can help you make better decisions: Data science techniques can help you analyse data and extract insights that can inform decision-making. This can be particularly useful in fields such as business, finance, and healthcare, where data-driven decision-making is becoming increasingly important.

Data science can lead to lucrative careers: Data science is well-paying, with data scientists earning high salaries and enjoying good job prospects. Learning data science can help you gain valuable skills in high demand and can be applied in various contexts.

It can also help you better understand and make sense of data and can lead to lucrative and fulfilling career opportunities. It is a perfect career choice for individuals with strong analytical and problem-solving skills who enjoy working with large amounts of data and are interested in applying these skills in various contexts.

And where to start?

To get started with data science, there are a few steps you can follow:

Familiarise yourself with programming: Data science involves working with large amounts of data, and programming languages such as Python and R are commonly used to manipulate, analyse, and visualise data. If you are new to programming, you may want to start by learning the basics of a programming language like Python or R.

Learn basic statistics and math: Data science involves applying statistical and mathematical concepts to data, so having a solid foundation in these areas is important. You may want to start by learning basic concepts such as mean, median, mode, standard deviation, and hypothesis testing.

Explore data visualisation tools: Visualising data can help you understand and communicate insights from your data. There are a variety of tools available for data visualisation, such as Matplotlib and Seaborn for Python and ggplot2 for R.

Practice working with real data: The best way to learn data science is to practice working with real data. Use the tools and techniques you have learned to explore the data, identify patterns and trends, and communicate your findings. You can find datasets online or use data from a personal project or hobby.

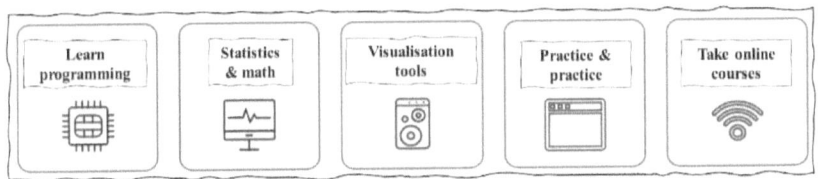

Figure 5 - Getting started with data science

Consider taking online courses or earning a degree: Many online courses and degree programs can help you learn data science. These can be a helpful way to gain a more in-depth understanding of data science concepts and techniques and provide you with the opportunity to learn from experienced professionals.

The key to learning data science is to be curious, practice frequently, and continue learning. As you gain more experience and knowledge, you can tackle more complex data science problems and projects.

Why it's highly paid?

Data scientists typically earn high salaries, as the demand for professionals with data science skills is high, and the field is relatively new and rapidly growing. According to data from Glassdoor, the median salary for a data scientist in the United States is $120,931 per year. However, salary can vary based on a variety of factors, including the specific industry, the company, the level of experience, and the location.

For example, data scientists in the technology industry may earn higher salaries than those in other industries, and data scientists in major cities like San Francisco and New York may earn higher salaries than those in other locations.

It's also worth noting that salaries for data scientists can vary depending on the specific role and responsibilities. For example, a data scientist with more experience or specialised skills may earn a higher salary than a data scientist with less experience or more general skills.

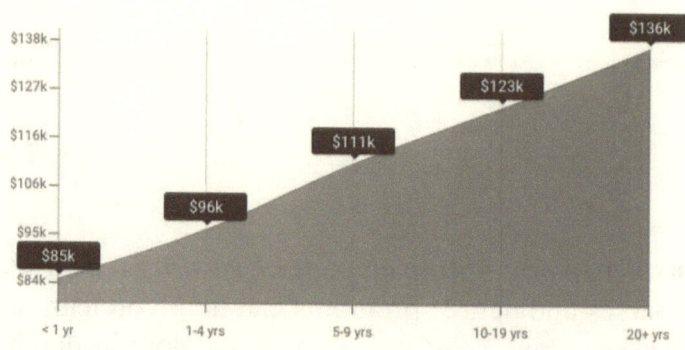

Figure 6 - Data science salaries by experience[1]

Overall, data science is well-paying, and data scientists can expect to earn high salaries, particularly as they gain more experience and specialised skills.

Where are the data science jobs?

Many companies hire data scientists, and the demand for professionals with data science skills is high across various industries. Some examples of companies that frequently hire data scientists to include:

Technology companies: Many tech companies, including Google, Amazon, and Microsoft, hire data scientists to work on various projects, such as developing machine learning models, analysing user data, and optimising algorithms.

Financial services companies: Data scientists are also in high demand in the financial services industry, where they can work on projects such as risk modelling, fraud detection, and customer segmentation.

Healthcare organisations: Data scientists are increasingly being hired by healthcare organisations to analyse large datasets and extract insights that can inform decision-making and improve patient care.

Consulting companies: Companies such as McKinsey, Bain, and BCG hire data scientists to work on projects for their clients.

Government agencies: Government agencies, including the National Institutes of Health (NIH) and the Centers for Disease Control and Prevention (CDC), also hire data scientists to work on projects related to public health and policy.

This is just a tiny sampling of companies that hire data scientists. Many other companies across various industries also hire data scientists, including retail, manufacturing, and transportation.

Why it's the future of jobs?

Data science is a rapidly growing field that is driving innovations in a variety of industries and is expected to continue to be a significant force in the future. Some reasons why data science is considered the future include:

Data is becoming increasingly important: The amount of data being generated and collected is growing exponentially, and data is becoming an increasingly important asset for businesses and organisations. As a result, there is a growing demand for professionals who can analyse and extract insights from data, and data science is well-positioned to meet this demand.

Data science is driving innovation: Data science is driving innovation in various fields, including healthcare, finance, technology, and more. Data scientists use data to develop new products and services, optimise business processes, and make more informed decisions.

Data science skills are in high demand: There is a high demand for professionals with data science skills, which is expected to continue. Data science skills are highly valued in the job market and can lead to lucrative and fulfilling career opportunities.

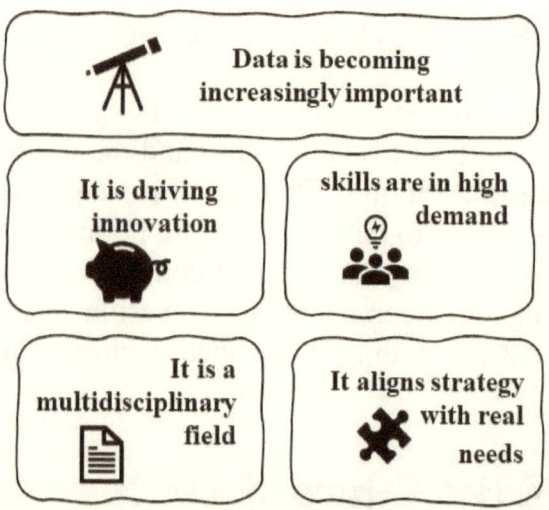

Figure 7 - Data science is the future of jobs

Data science is a multidisciplinary field: Data science involves combining concepts from a variety of fields, including computer science, statistics, and domain-specific expertise, which makes it an interdisciplinary field with a wide range of applications.

And why Artificial Intelligence?

Data science and artificial intelligence (AI) are two closely related fields that are driving innovations in various industries and are expected to continue to be significant forces in the future.

Data science involves using statistical and mathematical techniques to extract insights and value from large amounts of data. In contrast, AI consists in developing algorithms and systems that can perform tasks that would typically require human intelligence, such as learning, decision-making, and problem-solving.

In the future, data science and AI will continue to play a significant role in driving innovation and transforming industries. Some specific ways in which data science and AI are expected to shape the future include:

Enhancing decision-making: Data science and AI can help organisations make more informed and accurate decisions by providing insights and predictions based on data analysis.

Improving efficiency: Data science and AI can help organisations optimise processes and improve efficiency by automating tasks and identifying patterns and trends in data.

Developing new products and services: Data science and AI can create new products and services tailored to specific markets and customer needs.

Transforming industries: Data science and AI are expected to change various industries, including healthcare, finance, and transportation, by providing new insights and capabilities to drive innovation and improve outcomes.

Data science and AI are expected to play a major role in shaping the future and driving innovation in various industries.

How do companies use data?

OkCupid, Facebook, Amazon, Apple, and Google are all companies that collect and use data in various ways. Here are a few examples of how these companies use data:

OkCupid: OkCupid is a dating website that uses data to match users with potential partners. OkCupid collects data from user profiles and site activities and uses algorithms to match users based on their responses to questions and other data points.

Facebook: Facebook is a social media platform that uses data to personalise the content users see in their feeds and target ads. Facebook collects data from users' profiles, activities on the site, and interactions with other users and uses this data to tailor the content and ads that users see.

Amazon: Amazon is an e-commerce platform that uses data to personalise the user shopping experience and improve its operations. Amazon collects data from users' purchases and activities on the site and uses this data to recommend products to users and to optimise its supply chain and fulfilment processes.

Apple: Apple is a technology company that uses data to personalise the user experience and to improve its products and services. Apple collects data from users' interactions with its devices and services and uses this data to tailor the user experience and to inform the development of new products and features.

Google: Google is a technology company that uses data to personalise the user experience and to improve its products and services. Google collects data from users' searches and activities on its various platforms and uses this data to tailor the search results and ads that users see and to inform the development of new products and features.

These companies use data to personalise the user experience, improve operations, and drive innovation. We will explore more of these use cases later.

So what's in this book?

OK, now that you have a very generic understanding of data science, let's understand what we will learn in this book. With the knowledge you gain from this book, you will be better equipped to tackle data science problems.

Nowadays, learning data science doesn't need a thick textbook. Regardless of technical skill level, anyone may read and understand this book. Anybody who wants an easy entry into data science or wants to brush up on the fundamentals should read this book.

For clarity, particularly for newcomers, I've utilised simple language throughout. Included are such topics as "What is data science? " "How did data science come to be? " "Data science life cycle? " "Data science tools and technologies? " "Data science methodology? " "Data science models? " "Creating a data science business strategy? " "Managing data science projects? " "Data science roles? " and "Data science career path?" Knowledge of Python, R, databases, structure, artificial intelligence, machine learning, deep learning, neural networks, mathematical analysis, and statistical modelling is advantageous.

Some very elementary data science project concepts are presented here. Abbreviations used in data science, Data Science Tutorials Available for Free Online, plus much more.

Getting Started with Data Science

D ata science is the study of statistical and mathematical methods to analyse and understand real-world events through data. It combines techniques from various fields, such as mathematics, computer science, and statistics, and includes practices like machine learning, data engineering, image recognition, probability modelling, signal processing, and visualisation.

In recent years, data science has become essential to understanding how various industries function and has made significant progress.

Data science allows companies to analyse raw data and transform it into valuable insights to solve problems. It enables the discovery of hidden patterns and trends within the data, which can help organisations make better decisions.

Data science helps companies bring information to the surface and make more informed decisions. For example, Netflix uses data to understand viewer preferences and decide which shows to produce; Target uses data to identify key customer segments and understand their purchasing behaviour. Proctor and Gamble use data to forecast future demand and optimise production.

Data science definitions:

Data: Data refers to a collection of facts, such as numbers, words, measurements, observations or just descriptions of things. Data can be raw, unorganised facts that need to be processed or organised into a specific format, such as a database or spreadsheet.

Science: Science refers to the systematic and logical approach to discovering new knowledge, understanding the natural world, and explaining phenomena through observation, experimentation, and evidence-based reasoning. Science often involves collecting data, formulating hypotheses, testing predictions, and analysing and interpreting results.

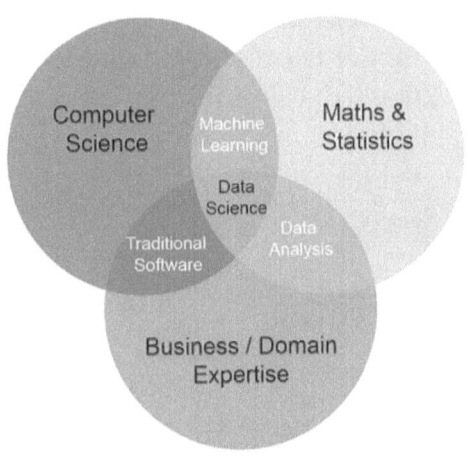

Figure 8 - Data science at the centre of attention

Data Science: In data science, data and science are combined to analyse and understand complex phenomena, make predictions and decisions, and solve problems. Data Science is a field that bridges the gap between data and information. It's about extracting knowledge from data and information, which can be used to solve complex problems. It's also about thinking differently and innovatively doing things.

Data scientists use various tools and techniques from computer science, statistics, and other fields to collect, process, and analyse large data sets to extract insights and knowledge that can inform decision-making and solve real-world problems.

The DIKW Model

Science is examining facts into a theory that has a degree. The basis used is the Data-Information-Knowledge-Wisdom (DIKW) hierarchy. The DIKW pyramid is also known as the DIKW hierarchy, the wisdom hierarchy, the knowledge hierarchy, the information hierarchy, and the data pyramid. Not all versions of the DIKW model reference the four components of science. The DIKW model is often cited and used to define data, information and knowledge in information management, information systems, and literature on knowledge management.

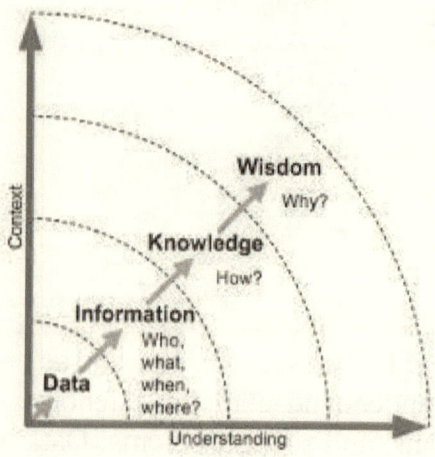

Figure 9 - The DIKW model of knowledge management

Data is a collection of raw facts and figures that can be processed and analysed to extract useful insights. Data can be numbers, words, measurements, observations, or other facts describing a particular phenomenon or situation.

Information is data that has been processed and organised to make it meaningful and useful. Information is derived from data through sorting, filtering, and aggregation processes, and it is often presented in a structured format, such as a report or database.

Knowledge is understanding or awareness of a particular subject or fact. It is derived from information through learning, analysis, and interpretation. Knowledge is often organised and structured and can be communicated and shared with others.

Wisdom is applying knowledge and understanding practically to make sound judgments and decisions. Wisdom is often considered a combination of knowledge and experience and is often associated with qualities such as insight, judgment, and discernment.

In summary, data is raw, unprocessed facts; information has been processed and organised; knowledge is understanding derived from information, and wisdom is applying knowledge and experience practically.

Fundamentals of data science

The fundamentals of data science include the following:

Programming: Data scientists use programming languages such as Python, R, and SQL to collect, clean, and analyse data.

Statistics: Data scientists use statistical techniques to understand patterns and make predictions based on that data.

Data visualisation: Data scientists use data visualisation tools to present data in a clear and easily understandable format, such as through charts, graphs, and maps.

Machine learning: Data scientists use machine learning algorithms to analyse data and make predictions or decisions without being explicitly programmed.

Data engineering: Data engineers build and maintain the systems and infrastructure that data scientists use to store, process, and analyse data.

Data management: Data management is collecting, organising, storing and retrieving data. It's an integral part of any data science job because it helps you ensure that your data is accurate, consistent and up-to-date. Data management tools include database management systems (DBMS), data warehouses (DW), and data marts (DM).

Data ethics: Data scientists should consider the ethical implications of their work, such as protecting user privacy and ensuring data is used responsibly.

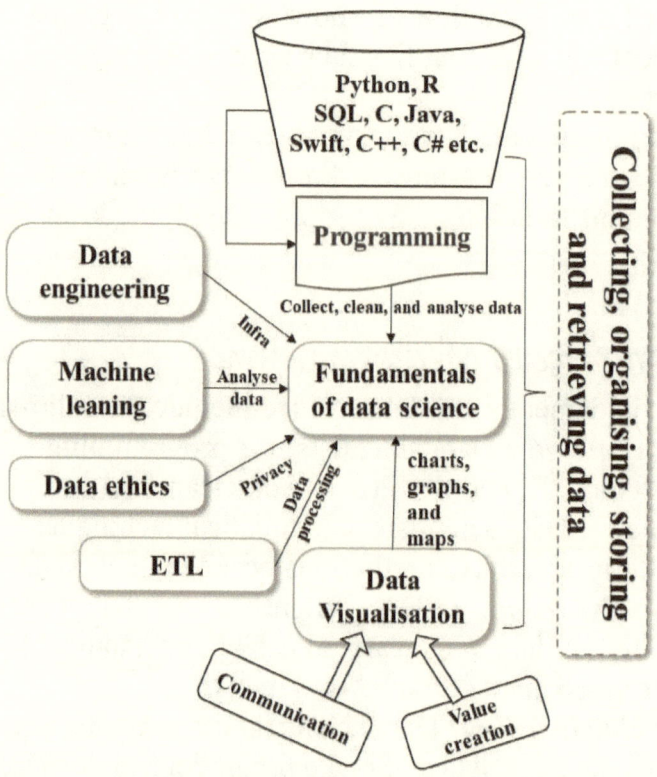

Figure 10 - The elements of data science

Communication: Data scientists must be able to effectively communicate their findings to various audiences, including technical and non-technical stakeholders.

Python: Python is a great place to start if you're interested in learning data science. It's an easy-to-use programming language with many powerful features for creating applications and websites. Python is used for machine learning, data analysis and scientific computing (among other things). The language has been around since 1991 and has gained popularity as an open-source software project—meaning anyone can use it free of charge!

R: R is a programming language developed at the University of Toronto and has become very popular among data scientists. It is used for data analysis, statistics, and machine learning. R's popularity stems from its ability to integrate seamlessly. R is free to use (open source) and supported by many universities world-wide, including Stanford University and Duke University.

SQL: SQL is a structured query language that defines how data can be queried and manipulated. It's used by many database management systems (DBMS), including MySQL, PostgreSQL and SQLite3. SQL is also commonly used in programming languages like PHP to query databases; if you're writing a web application that needs to interact with an existing database, you'll almost certainly use some flavour of SQL.

ETL (Extract, transform, load): ETL (Extract, Transform and Load) is a process of extracting data from one or more sources, transforming it into a format suitable for analysis, and loading it into a database. ETL plays an essential role in building large-scale analytics applications. ETL can be used to extract data from multiple sources and to transform the data into a form that can be easily analysed.

Data science methods

The range of methods of data science is vast. It includes very non-technical things such as written analyses and simple descriptive statistics, slightly more technical work such as data preparation and visualisation, or mathematically more complex things like predicting time series and automating human activities (such as pricing cinema tickets) – and much more.

Understanding that data science's ultimate goal is to solve a problem in a specific area is essential. Having said that, it is necessary to have a perfect knowledge of the field of application before embarking on developing a model. It should also be noted that the areas listed below do not represent an exhaustive list of disciplines involved in data science. In general, data science involves the following fields:

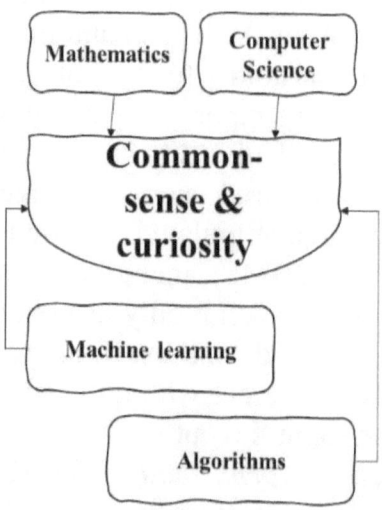

Figure 11 - Lots of common sense and curiosity are required for data science

The application area: The area of application is the sector (The environment) in which you want to make a data product or solve a problem. This could include, for example, the stock market if we're going to establish a predictive model for traders based on past stock prices.

Mathematics (Statistics, Probability, Linear Algebra, Analysis): Mathematics is a significant part of data science. Indeed, problems are very often translated into mathematical models before being solved.

Computer science: Computer science is the basis of data science because models are implemented with code and computer tools. Because data is digitally acquired, stored and processed through computing.

Machine learning: Machine learning techniques are increasingly being used in data science.

Algorithmics: Mastery of this science is essential since all models are in the form of algorithms. It is important to understand concepts such as complexity.

Common sense: This is, by far, what is most needed in the face of a complex problem. Of course, being a data scientist does not mean being an expert in all these areas (even if you have more knowledge in these areas, the better). Indeed, a data science project is often complex and consists of several steps. So, you can find people in a team with different profiles, each in charge of a specific step.

Lots of curiosity: Being curious is essential for data scientists because it allows them to ask questions, explore data, and look for patterns and insights that might not be immediately obvious. This curiosity drives data scientists to constantly seek new knowledge and ways to improve their understanding of the data they are working with. It also allows them to devise creative solutions to problems and explore new ways of using data to solve real-world problems.

In addition to being curious about the data itself, a data scientist should also be curious about the broader context in which the data is being used. This means being curious about the business or organisation that is using the data and the goals and objectives that the data is being used to support. This can help a data scientist to understand the broader context in which their work is being done and to develop more targeted and effective solutions.

All in all, being curious is an essential quality for data scientists because it helps them to learn and grow constantly, to think creatively and critically, and to approach their work with a sense of curiosity and a desire to understand the world around them.

The objectives of data science

The objectives of data science vary depending on the specific context and goals of a data science project. However, some common objectives of data science include the following:

Extracting insights and knowledge from data: Data scientists often use data to discover patterns, trends, and relationships that can help to understand a particular phenomenon or problem.

Making predictions and decisions: Data science can be used to build models that can predict future outcomes or recommend courses of action based on data.

Solving problems: Data science can be applied to a wide range of problems, such as identifying fraudulent activity, predicting customer behaviour, or optimising supply chain processes.

Communicating results: Data scientists often need to share their findings with stakeholders, such as business leaders, policymakers, or the general public. This may involve presenting results clearly and understandably through visualisations, reports, or other means.

So, the overall objectives of data science are to use data and analytical techniques to extract insights, make predictions and decisions, and solve problems that can positively impact business, society, or other areas.

The benefits of data science

Data science is an exciting field that allows us to answer questions we didn't know to ask. It's not just about crunching numbers, though: data scientists use their knowledge of data and machine learning to make predictions and improve our lives.

We have more data now than ever: Data is everywhere. We have more data now than ever before, and it's growing exponentially. In fact, we're producing more data than ever before and generating it faster than we can process it.

As a result of this rapid growth in the amount of digital information being created and stored by organisations around the world (e-commerce, social media posts & shares), there are new opportunities for businesses to harness this information for their own competitive advantage - and you don't need any special skills or technology infrastructure to do so! By combining your organisation's existing resources with advanced analytics tools like machine learning algorithms (ML), artificial intelligence (AI) systems like deep learning models/algorithms etc., you'll be able to make better decisions about what products/services customers want most, which will lead directly toward more incredible sales revenue growth over time.

Data is more accessible now than ever: Data is more accessible today than ever. Data has been democratised and made more accessible through open data, machine learning (ML), and cloud computing. Open data refers to information found on the internet or posted on social media platforms like Google Docs or Dropbox. This includes everything from weather reports to criminal records, and it's all free for anyone to access!

Finding the right data is half the battle: Data is everywhere, from social media to your email inbox and everyone's phone. The best way to find it is by asking questions or looking at trends that can help you understand how people behave in different situations. For example, if someone posts about how much they love their new pair of shoes on Instagram, you could use that information as an opportunity for market research.

You could create a campaign based on these insights, for example, sending a message directly to them via text, offering an exclusive discount code redeemable only within 24 hours of purchase (assuming they haven't already claimed their discount). This would be much more effective than advertising in traditional media channels because it taps directly into consumer interest rather than relying solely on brand awareness alone, and it also provides another layer of transparency that helps build trust between brands and consumers alike!

Data is being used in unexpected ways: As you can see, data science is being used in unforeseen ways. In fact, it's being used to make better decisions and products. We are also using data to improve our users' services and experiences.

Data can be a powerful tool for social good: It can improve public health, education and the environment by helping us understand how these systems work - and how they could work better. For example, data scientists have used big data sets to identify patterns in disease spread; public health officials then use this information to create new strategies for fighting disease outbreaks or reducing their prevalence rates.

Data scientists also have an increasing role in improving government services like education or environmental protection: they analyse large databases of student test scores from different schools, looking for those who show signs of learning disabilities before they even start preschool, or compare pollution levels at various locations around London or New York cities over time so that officials know when action must be taken (such as closing down factories).

By applying advanced analytical techniques such as machine learning algorithms along with detailed datasets about different groups' needs/preferences/demographics etc., we can begin making decisions based on real-world evidence rather than opinions alone

Data science is a way of thinking about problems you never thought about before. It's also a way to solve problems or make them manageable. If you've ever had a question but lacked the resources or knowledge to answer it, data science may help you.

Data science is a powerful tool for answering questions we didn't know to ask. In this blog post, we've explored ways that data can be used unexpectedly to solve problems and improve our lives. For example, by bringing reliable information about the world closer to people who need it most, we can empower people who otherwise feel isolated from society. We also showed how data science allows us to answer questions about our environment that were previously impossible or too expensive to do, like understanding climate change better than ever. Finally, let's not forget how important data is when it comes down to helping others: making sure nobody goes hungry anymore because they lack access to food or shelter; creating opportunities so that children can access education without fear of being bullied; providing support for people with disabilities by allowing them more independence within their communities; all these things rely on having good quality data available at all times.

Disadvantages of data science

There are a few potential disadvantages of data science to consider:

Data quality: The accuracy and reliability of data science insights and predictions depend on the quality of the data being analysed. If the data is incomplete, incorrect, or biased, the results of data science analyses may be flawed.

Ethical considerations: Data science can raise ethical concerns, such as privacy violations or discrimination. Data scientists must consider their work's potential ethical implications and ensure that data is collected, used, and shared responsibly.

Complexity: Data science can be a complex field requiring specialised knowledge and skills in areas such as computer science, statistics, and machine learning. This can make it challenging for organisations to find and hire qualified data scientists. It can also make it difficult for data scientists to stay up-to-date with the latest techniques and technologies.

Resource intensive: Data science projects can be resource-intensive, requiring significant time and financial investment. Organisations may need to invest in specialised hardware and software and hire and train personnel to carry out data science projects.

While data science can bring many benefits, it is essential to carefully consider the potential disadvantages and ensure that data science is applied ethically and responsibly.

How to get over the disadvantages?

There are a few steps that organisations can take to consider the potential disadvantages of data science:

Assess the data quality: Data quality is an essential factor in the reliability of data science insights and predictions. Organisations should carefully assess the data quality, including its completeness, accuracy, and bias.

Consider ethical implications: Data science can raise ethical concerns, such as privacy violations or discrimination. It is important for organisations to consider the potential ethical implications of their data science projects and to ensure that data is collected, used, and shared responsibly.

Invest in training and resources: Data science can be complex, requiring specialised knowledge and skills. Organisations should invest in training and resources to ensure that their data science teams have the necessary skills and knowledge to carry out their work effectively.

Plan for resource requirements: Data science projects can be resource-intensive, requiring significant time and financial investment. Organisations should carefully plan for these requirements and allocate sufficient resources to ensure the success of their data science projects.

In fact, by carefully considering the potential disadvantages of data science and taking steps to address them, organisations can ensure that they are able to maximise the benefits of data science while minimising potential risks.

What are the other challenges?

Learning and writing code: This is one of the significant disadvantages of data science, but it can also be overcome by being open-minded about what you're learning and being willing to work with others. Learning a new language will take time if you're new to programming. You'll probably also want guidance from someone who knows more than you do—a mentor or coach can help ensure that your skills are up-to-date and professional before moving on in life.

Working with data quality: As a data scientist, you will likely work with many different data types. For example, I might be given some raw text from an article and asked to analyse its sentiment analysis algorithms. Or perhaps I can access a database full of purchase transactions for goods at my company's retail locations. Either way, cleaning up these datasets can be time-consuming and difficult.

The problem of data sparsity: The problem is that there is not enough data to make a valid prediction. This can be solved by collecting more training data, which will help your model learn how to make correct predictions based on more examples.

- To collect more training data, you can use different methods, including:
- Crowdsourcing (i.e., asking your friends and family for help)
- Surveys (i.e., asking people who have similar interests or habits as those in the dataset)

The importance of data security: Data security is a top priority for any business, but it's not always easy to implement. Data science projects can be expensive and time-consuming, requiring a lot of research into the best way to secure your data.

Data security should be included in every decision you make about your data science project, from choosing which tool(s) you will use to determining whether or not you need a certifiable professional on board as an employee or contractor.

Finding the right person to fill the role: You need a solid grasp of math, statistics and computer science. You also need to have an eye for data visualisation and be able to communicate your findings clearly. Data scientists are often problem solvers; they collect information and interpret the results to come up with solutions that will benefit the company or organisation they work for. In order to find someone who fits these requirements, you should consider asking yourself some questions:

- Do I want someone who has been trained as a scientist or mathematician?
- Do I want someone who has had experience working with large amounts of data before?

As I mentioned earlier, data science is a hot field, so finding good talent for these jobs can be challenging, but it is a great career for someone who enjoys learning and working with data. To get into data analysis, start by looking at online courses or reading books on the topic. You need to be able to work with data and learn new skills, so consider taking statistics or machine learning classes.

The beauty of data science is that it combines the best parts of both computer science and statistics. It's a field where you can spend your time learning new things and contributing to the world while also making money. If this sounds like something that might be right for you, then there are many ways to find a job in our industry. But first, let's get more knowledge about data science.

Where is data science used now?

Data science is used in many industries to extract insights, make predictions and decisions, and solve problems. Some examples of how data science is used across different industries include:

Agriculture: Data science optimises agricultural practices, predicts crop yields, and improves food security.

Healthcare: Data science can analyse medical records and other healthcare data to identify trends and patterns, predict outcomes, and optimise treatment plans.

Finance: Data science can be used to analyse financial data and predict market trends, identify fraudulent activity, and optimise investment strategies.

Retail: Data science can be used to analyse customer data and behaviour to inform marketing and sales strategies, optimise inventory management, and improve the customer experience.

Manufacturing: Data science can be used to optimise production processes, predict equipment failures, and improve supply chain efficiency.

Transportation: Data science can be used to optimise routes, predict demand, and improve safety in the transportation industry.

Education: Data science can be used to analyse student data and predict academic performance, optimise class schedules, and improve the effectiveness of education programs.

The History of Data Science

The history of data science is long and complex, involving contributions from a wide range of disciplines, and it continues to evolve as new technologies and techniques are developed. Data science history spans many centuries and involves contributions from various disciplines. Some key milestones in the history of data science include:

Ancient history

Data science can be traced back to ancient civilisations that used statistical techniques to analyse data and make decisions. For example, the ancient Egyptians used a system of hieroglyphics to record and analyse data, which I also briefly touched on at the opening of this book. The ancient Greeks used geometry and mathematics to understand the natural world.

The system of hieroglyphics

The system of hieroglyphics was a set of pictorial symbols to record and communicate information. The ancient Egyptians used hieroglyphics for a variety of purposes, including record-keeping, communication, and artistic expression.

The ancient Egyptians used them for financial, legal, and administrative records. They also used hieroglyphics to record historical events, such as wars, battles, and significant achievements.

In addition to recording data, the ancient Egyptians also used hieroglyphics to analyse and interpret data. For example, they used hieroglyphics to track agricultural production, record census data, and track the movements of people and goods.

Columns or horizontal lines are used to write in hieroglyphs. Typically, they are read from top to bottom and right to left. The script may occasionally be read from left to right. For instance, the text should be read from right to left if a figure is facing the right. The animal and human representations, which face the text's commencement, might help the reader discern the orientation.

Figure 12 - Hieroglyphics writing

Overall, the ancient Egyptians used a system of hieroglyphics to record and analyse a wide range of data, which played a critical role in the administration and management of their civilisation.

The use of ancient geometry Greeks

The ancient Greeks made significant contributions to geometry and mathematics and used these fields to understand and explain the natural world.

Geometry, the study of shapes and spatial relationships, was developed by the ancient Greeks to understand and describe the physical world. The ancient Greeks used geometry to measure and describe objects' properties and make predictions about the outcomes of different scenarios.

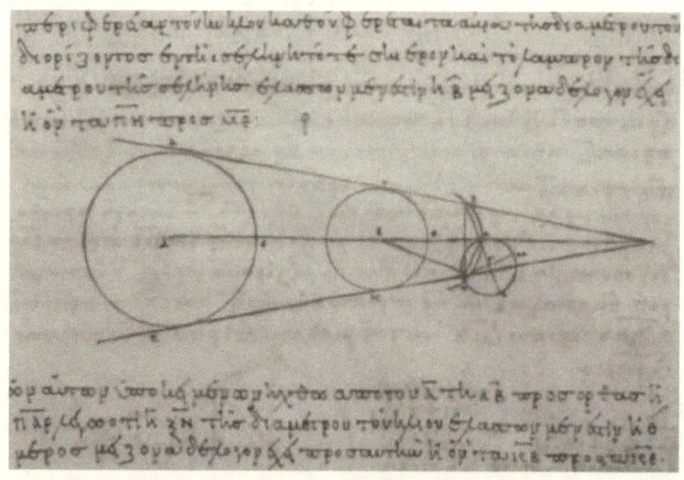

Figure 13 - The use of geometry by ancient Greeks

Mathematics, which is the study of numbers, quantities, and shapes, was also developed by the ancient Greeks as a way to understand and describe the natural world. The ancient Greeks used mathematics to make calculations, understand patterns and relationships, and predict outcomes.

The ancient Greeks used geometry and mathematics to understand and explain a wide range of phenomena, including the movements of the celestial bodies, the properties of shapes and figures, and the relationships between quantities. Their work in these fields laid the foundation for today's mathematical and geometric concepts.

The 1950s and 1960s

The term "data science" was coined in the 1950s by statistician John Tukey, and computer science also emerged as a discipline around this time. The combination of these two fields and the increasing availability of computers and data paved the way for the development of data science as we know it today.

John Tukey was a data analysis pioneer and contributed significantly to developing statistical methods and techniques for analysing data.

Tukey is best known for his work in the field of exploratory data analysis, which involves using statistical techniques to identify patterns, trends, and relationships in data. He is also credited with developing the concept of data-driven decision-making, which involves using data and statistical analysis to inform business and policy decisions.

Figure 14 - John Tukey

Tukey's work had a significant impact on the field of data science, and his contributions are still widely recognised and respected today. Tukey is often considered one of the pioneers of data science and is credited with helping to establish data science as a discipline in its own right.

The 1950s also marked a significant milestone in developing computer science as a discipline. The 1950s saw the development of the first high-level programming languages, which made it easier for programmers to write code and made it possible to develop more complex software. The 1950s also saw the development of the first commercial computers, which paved the way for the growth of the computer industry in the decades that followed.

Figure 15 - Early computers (the 1940s - 1960s)

The first computers were developed in the 1930s and 1940s, and they were large, expensive machines used primarily for scientific and military applications. These early computers were used to perform calculations and process data, and they were built using various technologies, such as vacuum tubes and electromechanical switches.

Several organisations and institutions developed the first computers, including government agencies and universities. Some early pioneers in computer science include John Atanasoff, who developed the first electronic computer in the 1930s, and John Mauchly and J. Presper Eckert, who developed the first general-purpose computer, known as the ENIAC, in the 1940s.

The development of the first computers marked a major milestone in the history of data science and paved the way for the computer industry's growth in the following decades.

While the 1950s marked an important milestone in the development of computer science, the field has a long history that stretches back to the early 20th century.

The early 20th century

The field of statistics emerged as a discipline in the early 20th century, with the development of statistical methods for analysing data and making predictions. This laid the foundation for many of the techniques used in data science today.

Figure 16 - Sir William Petty, a 17th-century economist who used early statistical methods to analyse demographic data

In the early 20th century, the field of data science began to take shape as a discipline in its own right. Some key milestones in the early 20th century that contributed to the development of data science include:

The rise of statistics: The early 20th century saw the development of statistical methods for analysing data and making predictions. This included the development of statistical techniques such as correlation analysis and regression analysis, which are still widely used in data science today.

The development of computer science: The field of computer science also emerged as a discipline in the early 20th century, with the development of the first computers and the development of programming languages such as FORTRAN and COBOL.

The emergence of big data: The early 20th century saw the emergence of large-scale data sets, such as the United States Census, which required new tools and techniques to manage and analyse. This led to the development of new statistical methods and the emergence of new fields, such as demography and social statistics.

The early 20th century certainly laid the foundation for many of today's techniques and technologies used in data science. It marked the beginning of a new era of data-driven decision-making and analysis.

The late 20th century

In the late 20th century, the proliferation of computers and the emergence of the internet led to the growth of big data, which required new tools and techniques to manage and analyse large amounts of data. This led to the developing of technologies such as Hadoop and new data-driven industries, such as digital marketing and e-commerce.

The late 20th century was a significant period in the history of data science, as it saw the proliferation of computers and the emergence of the internet, which led to the growth of big data and the development of new tools and techniques for managing and analysing large amounts of data. Some key milestones in the late 20th century that contributed to the development of data science include:

The growth of big data: The late 20th century saw the emergence of large-scale data sets, such as the United States Census, which required new tools and techniques to manage and analyse. This led to the development of new statistical methods and the emergence of new fields, such as demography and social statistics.

The development of machine learning: In the latter part of the 20th century, machine learning techniques, such as artificial neural networks, enabled computers to learn from data and make predictions without being explicitly programmed to do so.

The proliferation of computers and the internet: The late 20th century saw the proliferation of computers and the emergence of the internet, which made it easier to collect, store, and analyse data. This led to the growth of data-driven industries, such as digital marketing and e-commerce.

The late 20th century was a significant period in the history of data science, as it saw the growth of big data and the development of new tools and techniques for managing and analysing large amounts of data.

The 21st century

In the 21st century, data science has become an increasingly important field with the proliferation of data-driven technologies such as machine learning and artificial intelligence. Data science has become a key driver of innovation and decision-making in many industries and is now considered a critical discipline for the digital age.

The 21st century has seen the continued growth of big data, with the proliferation of data-generating technologies, such as the internet of things (IoT) and mobile devices, leading to an explosion of data. This has led to the development new tools and techniques for managing and analysing large amounts of data, such as Hadoop and NoSQL databases.

The 21st century has seen the continued development and advancement of machine learning technologies, such as deep learning, which has enabled computers to learn from data and make predictions and decisions with high accuracy.

The 21st century has seen the growth of data-driven industries, such as digital marketing and e-commerce, as well as the emergence of new data-driven applications in a wide range of industries, including healthcare, finance, and transportation.

From data analysis to data science

In 1996, Usama Fayyad[2], Gregory Piatetsky-Shapiro[3] and Padhraic Smyth[4] published the book *"From Data Mining to Knowledge Discovery in Databases"*. The authors say that historically, finding functional patterns in data has received many names, including data mining, knowledge mining, information discovery, data collection, data archaeology, and data patterns. Throughout the 2000s, various scientific journals began recognising data science as an evolving discipline. In 2005, the National Science Council supported the career development of data science professionals to ensure experts' availability.

By this time, companies have also begun to view data as a commodity to make money on. In a 2005 report by the Babson College Working Knowledge Research Centre, Thomas Davenport, Don Cohen and Al Jacobson wrote that instead of competing on traditional factors, companies are beginning to use statistical and quantitative analysis and predictive modelling as key competition elements.

In 2009, Google chief economist Hal Varian told McKinsey quarterly that he was concerned about the lack of data to analyse "free and ubiquitous data" of people.

Modern data science

In 2010, Drew Conway[5] published a book in which he wrote that someone who wants to become a competent data scientist has a lot to learn. Unfortunately, simply listing texts and textbooks does not untangle the knots. As data science evolves and becomes part of the business, so does the need to build strong innovation teams in this area. In 2011, D.J. Patil[6] published an article entitled "Creating a Data Science Team." He explains what skills, perspectives, tools and processes make such teams successful. In 2021, data science became central to IT amid significant technological advances as more consumers began to master them at lightning speed.

Usama Fayyad

Gregory Piatetsky-Shapiro

Padhraic Smyth

Hal Varian

Drew Conway

Dhanurjay "DJ" Patil

With higher processing speeds than ever, technology has made a giant leap into the new decade. Big data, machine learning and deep learning, are central to almost all industries, from business to education and medicine. Today, Data Science specialists are invaluable to any company.

We see that data science's roots lie in statistics and rely on mathematics and computer science. Data science also stems from the practical purpose of using the information to gain knowledge, particularly the idea of using data to solve business problems, as I have stated a few times already.

Data science will continue to change as human needs change, but one point remains clear, data scientists will be in demand as long as data needs to be analysed. The question is how much data will be available, where it will come from, and what new analysis methods will give them an even deeper understanding.

Data Science Framework

Data scientists can use many different frameworks when working with data. But since this is a beginner's guide to data science, we will stick to the simplest one. It includes the steps and processes that data scientists follow in order to extract insights and value from data.

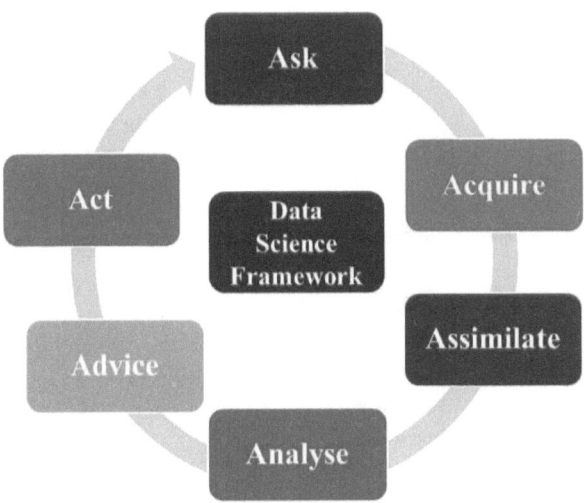

Figure 17 - Data Science Framework

If the process of translating data into action is known as data science, then the overarching framework will be comprised of the following seven high-level steps:

- Ask
- Acquire
- Assimilate
- Analyse
- Answer
- Advise

- Act

Asking Questions

Data science starts by asking questions and then uses the responses to provide guidance and take action. Like any intelligent scientist, a data scientist should be curious and be able to ask and respond to questions in addition to having a formal foundation in mathematics. Assumptions made along the route should be able to be rigorously examined by the data to determine whether the conclusions reached are sound.

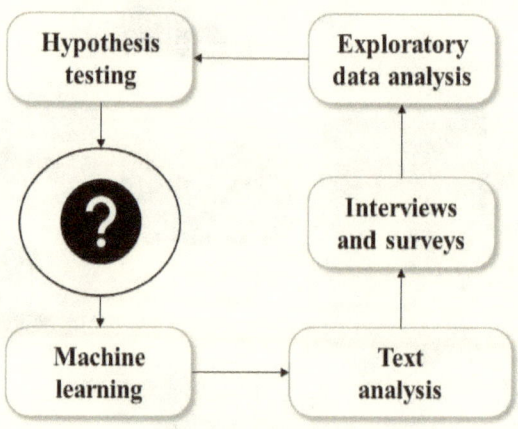

Figure 18 - Methods used for asking questions

Asking questions is an integral part of the scientific method and is central to the process of data science. When data scientists try to solve a problem, they need to understand the context of the problem and the data they are working with. This often involves asking many questions to clarify their understanding of the problem and identify the most relevant data to use in their analysis.

Asking questions also helps a data scientist to think critically about the problem and to come up with creative solutions. By asking questions and constantly seeking to learn more about the problem, data scientists can uncover new insights and perspectives that can inform their analysis and decision-making.

In data science, it is important to be curious about the data and the questions it can help to answer. This curiosity can help a data scientist to identify patterns and trends in the data and to come up with creative solutions to problems. On the other hand, curiosity is an essential trait for data scientists because it drives their desire to understand and explore data.

Additionally, curiosity helps data scientists stay up-to-date on new developments in the field and continuously learn and improve their skills. Being curious and open to new ideas and approaches in a rapidly-evolving field like data science is important.

Methods used for asking questions

There are several methods that data scientists use for asking questions in data science:

Hypothesis testing: This involves formulating a hypothesis about a relationship between variables and testing it using statistical analysis.

Exploratory data analysis: This involves visually examining the data to identify patterns and trends and generate further research ideas.

Interviews and surveys: These methods involve collecting data through direct communication with individuals or groups.

Text analysis: This involves using natural language processing techniques to analyse unstructured text data, such as social media posts or customer reviews.

Machine learning: This involves training algorithms to identify patterns in data and make predictions or decisions based on those patterns.

Overall, data scientists use a combination of these methods to ask and answer questions using data.

Acquiring data

The task of a data scientist is to identify the inputs or features that will make data mining, pattern recognition, and machine learning algorithms effective.

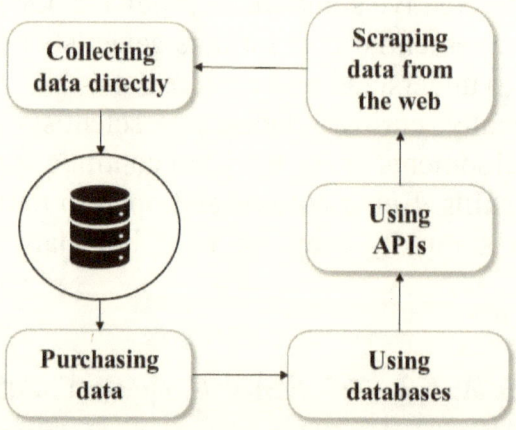

Figure 19 - Methods for acquiring data

A data scientist will attempt to gather the necessary data and synthesise it into usable form after posing a series of questions. The process of selecting the elements is known as feature engineering.

Once the components have been established, acquiring the data may be as easy as downloading it from a public data source or building a collaborative framework to record or measure data. Data needs to be cleaned and changed after it has been gathered. Dealing with missing values, erroneous values, and probable outliers typically falls under this step.

Methods for acquiring data

There are several methods that data scientists use for acquiring data in data science:

Collecting data directly: involves collecting data from sensors, experiments, or surveys.

Scraping data from the web: This involves using tools to extract data from websites or other online sources.

Using APIs: Many websites and services provide APIs (Application Programming Interfaces) that allow data to be accessed and extracted programmatically.

Using databases: Data scientists may also access and extract data from databases, such as relational databases or NoSQL databases.

Purchasing data from third parties: Data may be obtained from commercial data providers or other organisations selling data.

Assimilating data

Assimilating data refers to combining data from various sources and integrating it into a single, cohesive dataset. This process is often an essential step in data science, as it allows data scientists to analyse data from multiple sources and gain a more comprehensive understanding of the problem they are trying to solve.

Methods used for assimilation of data

There are several steps involved in assimilating data:

Data acquisition: The first step is to obtain the data from various sources. This may involve collecting data directly, scraping data from the web, using APIs, accessing databases, or purchasing data from third parties.

Data cleaning: Once the data has been acquired, it is often necessary to clean the data to remove errors, inconsistencies, or missing values.

Data transformation: The data may also need to be transformed to a consistent format, such as converting text data to numerical data or aggregating data at a different level of granularity.

Data integration: After the data has been cleaned and transformed, it can be integrated into a single dataset. This may involve merging multiple datasets or combining data from different sources.

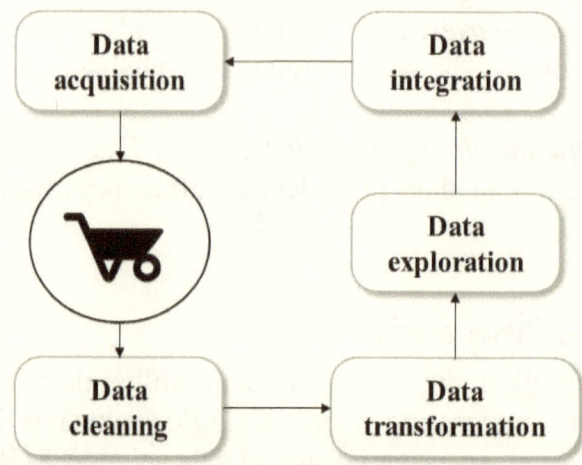

Figure 20 - Methods used for assimilation of data

Data exploration: After the data has been assimilated, scientists may explore it to understand its characteristics better and identify trends or patterns.

Essentially, assimilating data is an essential step in data science that involves acquiring, cleaning, transforming, and integrating data from various sources.

Analysing Data

Data analysis is the process of gathering, modelling, and evaluating data to derive knowledge that supports decision-making. Depending on the sector and the research objective, there are several ways and procedures for conducting analysis.

In science, data analysis employs a more sophisticated methodology and cutting-edge techniques to investigate and experiment with data. But in a corporate setting, data is used to support data-driven decisions that can boost an organisation's productivity. We will look into more details on data analysis in this book later.

Methods used in analysing data

Many methods are used for data analysis, including:

Statistical analysis: This involves using statistical techniques to analyse data and draw conclusions. Examples include hypothesis testing, regression analysis, and ANOVA.

Machine learning: This involves using algorithms to learn patterns in data and make predictions or decisions based on those patterns. Examples include decision trees, random forests, and support vector machines.

Data visualisation: This involves using charts, plots, and other visualisations to explore and understand data. Examples include bar plots, scatter plots and heatmaps.

Text analysis: This involves using natural language processing techniques to analyse unstructured text data, such as social media posts or customer reviews.

Network analysis: This involves analysing data organised as a network, such as a social network or a transportation network.

Spatial analysis: This involves analysing data that has a geographic component, such as location data or data related to the physical environment.

Answering Questions with data

Since there are many features (inputs) and the data has a variance, it is expected that the model will have some fundamental error and suffer from bias and variance. Therefore, after we build a model with the data, we need to evaluate if the model is performing well, and then tune the model, choose another model or combine the model until we have the desired performance. We will then be able to answer the question with data with a proper model.

We must always keep in mind that even if data is gathered, it is not always accurate, and correlations discovered in the data do not always imply causality because there are many other factors at play. This entire process, from the exploratory data to modelling and evaluation, is known as data mining; we will learn more about this later.

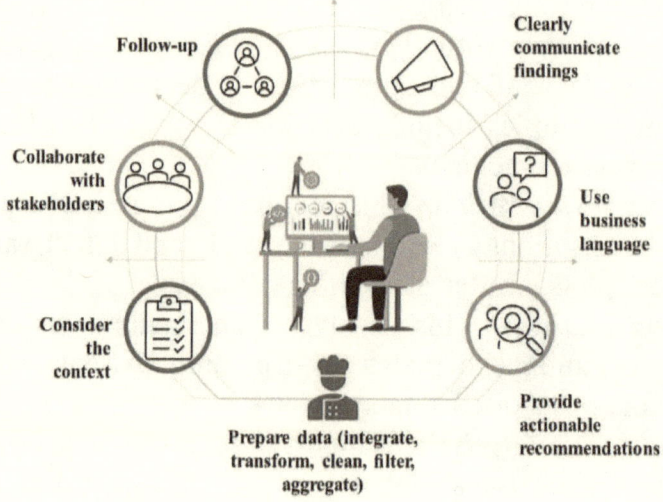

Figure 21 - Advise and act principles

Advise and Act

The advise stage is a crucial (and much overlooked) aspect of data science. After comprehending the data, a data scientist must offer advice that can be put into practice. Project economics, simulation, optimisation, and decision-making under uncertainty are used to accomplish this.

There are several ways that data scientists can offer advice that can be put into practice:

Clearly communicate findings: Data scientists should present their results clearly and concisely, using visuals and examples to help explain their recommendations.

Use business language: Data scientists should use language that is easy for non-technical stakeholders to understand rather than technical jargon.

Provide actionable recommendations: Data scientists should provide specific recommendations for implementing their findings rather than just presenting the data.

Consider the context: Data scientists should consider the business context and constraints when offering advice and tailor their recommendations accordingly.

Collaborate with stakeholders: Data scientists should work closely with stakeholders to ensure their recommendations are feasible and align with business goals.

Follow-up: Data scientists should follow up on their recommendations to ensure they are being implemented and provide additional support.

How does a business need to act?

It is important for businesses to carefully consider the findings and recommendations presented by data scientists, as these insights can inform decision-making and drive business strategy. Here are some steps that businesses can take to act on the findings presented by data scientists:

Review the findings and recommendations: Carefully review the findings and recommendations presented by the data scientists, and ask questions to clarify any points that are not understood.

Assess the feasibility and potential impact of the recommendations: Consider the resources, time, and budget required to implement the recommendations, as well as the potential impact on the business.

Prioritise the recommendations: Determine which recommendations are most important and should be implemented based on their potential impact and feasibility.

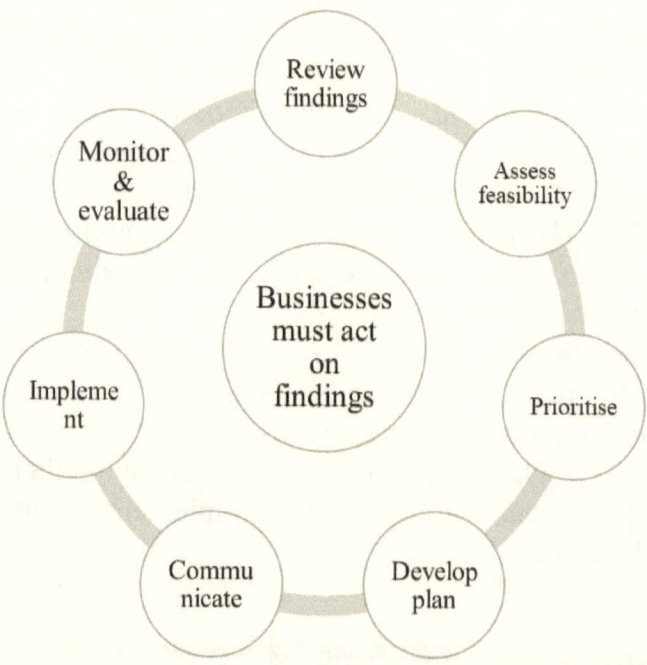

Figure 22 - Actions businesses must undertake after data insight results

Develop a plan to implement the recommendations: Create a plan that outlines the steps needed to implement the recommendations, including who will be responsible for each step and any resources that will be required.

Communicate the plan to relevant stakeholders: Share the plan with all relevant stakeholders, including the data scientists, to ensure that everyone knows the proposed actions and their implementation roles.

Implement the recommendations: Follow the plan to implement the recommendations and track progress to ensure that the recommendations are being effectively implemented.

Monitor and evaluate the results: Once the recommendations have been implemented, monitor and evaluate the results to determine their impact and make any necessary adjustments.

Data Science Roles

Working with data is a meta talent; one must possess various abilities to succeed in this field. Even if this opens up many opportunities, hunting for a job might become stressful.

Companies hire for various data science positions, and each of these positions calls for a specific set of skills. Here we will explore what each data professional does and how their contributions to a company vary depending on their job description.

Figure 23 - Different key roles in data science

Several roles are commonly associated with data science, including:

Data Strategist

A data strategist is responsible for developing and implementing a data strategy that aligns with an organisation's overall goals and objectives. This may involve working with stakeholders to understand their data needs and priorities and developing plans and frameworks for collecting, storing, and analysing data.

Some specific tasks that a data strategist may be responsible for include:

- Identifying opportunities to use data to drive business value
- Developing a roadmap for implementing data-driven initiatives
- Defining key performance indicators and metrics for tracking the success of data initiatives
- Collaborating with data scientists and other data professionals to develop and implement data solutions
- Ensuring that data governance and privacy policies are in place and followed
- Developing and implementing training programs to help employees understand how to use data effectively
- Communicating the data strategy and its progress to stakeholders within the organisation.

A data strategist may also be responsible for managing budgets and resources related to data initiatives and staying up-to-date on industry trends and best practices in data management and analysis.

Domain Expert

A domain expert is a person who has a deep understanding of a particular field or subject area. In the context of data science, a domain expert is someone who has extensive knowledge and expertise in a specific industry or application area and can provide valuable insights and guidance to data scientists and other team members working on data-driven projects in that domain.

For example, a domain expert in healthcare might be a physician or nurse with a deep understanding of medical terminology, processes, and protocols. A domain expert in finance might be an investment banker with a strong knowledge of financial markets and products.

Domain experts are often consulted by data scientists and other team members to help them understand the context and terminology of the data they are working with and to provide guidance on how to interpret and use the data to solve problems and make informed decisions. Domain experts may also be involved in defining the goals and objectives of data-driven projects and in reviewing and providing feedback on the results and recommendations of those projects.

Business Translator

A business translator is responsible for translating business-related documents and materials from one language to another. This may include marketing materials, financial reports, contracts, and other documents.

Some specific responsibilities of a business translator may include the following:

- Translating business-related documents and materials from one language to another, ensuring that the translations accurately convey the original meaning
- Proofreading and editing translations to ensure that they are grammatically correct and free of errors
- Working with translation software and other tools to ensure that translations are consistent and accurate
- Researching industry-specific terminology and concepts to ensure that translations are accurate and up-to-date

- Collaborating with clients and team members to ensure that translations meet their needs and expectations
- Staying up-to-date with developments in the business world and with translation best practices

Business translators typically work in various industries, including finance, marketing, and consulting. They may work for a translation agency, consulting companies, or in-house at a business or organisation.

Data Scientist

A data scientist is a professional who uses statistical and machine learning techniques to analyse and interpret data and develops models and algorithms to solve problems and make predictions. Data scientists work with large and complex datasets and are responsible for extracting insights and value from the data to inform business decisions and drive innovation.

Some specific tasks that a data scientist may be responsible for include:

- Collecting and preparing data for analysis, including acquiring data from various sources and cleaning and preprocessing the data
- Exploring and analysing data to identify trends, patterns, and relationships
- Building and evaluating statistical and machine learning models to solve problems and make predictions
- Communicating findings and recommendations to stakeholders through reports, presentations, and visualisations
- Implementing data-driven solutions and tracking their performance

- Staying up-to-date on industry trends and best practices in data science and continually learning new techniques and tools

Data scientists may work in a variety of industries, including finance, healthcare, retail, and technology. They may be involved in a wide range of projects, including predictive modelling, customer segmentation, fraud detection, and more.

Data Architect

A data architect is responsible for designing and implementing an organisation's data infrastructure and systems. This includes designing and building databases and data models and defining the relationships between different data elements.

Some specific tasks that a data architect may be responsible for include:

- Defining the overall data architecture of an organisation, including the data model, data storage systems, and data flow
- Collaborating with data scientists, data engineers, and other stakeholders to understand their data needs and requirements
- Developing and implementing data management policies and procedures
- Designing and implementing data pipelines and ETL processes to ensure that data is accurately and efficiently transferred between systems
- Ensuring that data is secure and compliant with relevant regulations and policies
- Evaluating and selecting appropriate technologies and tools for data management and analysis
- Managing budgets and resources related to data architecture and infrastructure.

A data architect may also be responsible for staying up-to-date on industry trends and best practices in data management and helping educate other team members on data architecture principles and techniques.

Data Engineer

A data engineer is a professional who designs and builds the infrastructure and systems needed to store, process and analyse large volumes of data. Data engineers work closely with data scientists and other stakeholders to understand their data needs and requirements and develop solutions to meet those needs.

Some specific tasks that a data engineer may be responsible for include:

- Designing and building data pipelines to extract, transform, and load data from various sources
- Developing and maintaining data storage systems, including databases, data lakes, and data warehouses
- Ensuring that data is accurate and up-to-date and that data integrity is maintained
- Implementing data governance and security policies and procedures
- Optimising the performance and scalability of data systems
- Collaborating with data scientists and other stakeholders to understand their data needs and requirements
- Staying up-to-date on industry trends and best practices in data engineering and continually learning new technologies and tools

Data engineers may work in a variety of industries, including finance, healthcare, retail, and technology. They may be involved in a wide range of projects, including data warehousing, data lake implementation, and data pipeline development.

Data Analyst

A data analyst is a professional who collects, organises, and analyses data to inform business decisions. Data analysts work with large and complex datasets and use statistical techniques and visualisation tools to uncover trends and patterns in the data. They may also be responsible for communicating their findings and recommendations to stakeholders.

Some specific tasks that a data analyst may be responsible for include:

- Collecting and preparing data for analysis, including acquiring data from various sources and cleaning and preprocessing the data
- Exploring and analysing data to identify trends, patterns, and relationships
- Using statistical techniques and visualisation tools to uncover insights from the data
- Communicating findings and recommendations to stakeholders through reports, presentations, and visualisations
- Developing dashboards and reports to track key performance indicators and metrics
- Collaborating with data scientists and other stakeholders to understand their data needs and requirements
- Staying up-to-date on industry trends and best practices in data analysis and continually learning new techniques and tools

Data analysts may work in a variety of industries, including finance, healthcare, retail, and technology, and may be involved in a wide range of projects, including customer segmentation, fraud detection, and predictive modelling.

Machine Learning Engineer

A machine learning engineer is a professional who builds and implements machine learning models and algorithms. Machine learning engineers work with data scientists and other stakeholders to understand their data needs and requirements and develop solutions to meet those needs using machine learning techniques.

Some specific tasks that a machine learning engineer may be responsible for include:

- Building and implementing machine learning models and algorithms
- Optimising the performance of machine learning models
- Integrating machine learning models into production systems
- Collaborating with data scientists and other stakeholders to understand their data needs and requirements
- Staying up-to-date on industry trends and best practices in machine learning and continually learning new techniques and tools
- Managing budgets and resources related to machine learning projects
- Tracking and analysing the performance of machine learning models to identify areas for improvement

Machine learning engineers may work in a variety of industries, including finance, healthcare, retail, and technology, and may be involved in a wide range of projects, including predictive modelling, natural language processing, and computer vision.

Business Intelligence Analyst

A business intelligence (BI) analyst uses data and analysis to support decision-making and strategic planning within an organisation. BI analysts work with large and complex datasets and use tools and techniques such as dashboards, reports, and visualisations to uncover insights and trends that inform business decisions.

Some specific tasks that a BI analyst may be responsible for include:

- Collecting and preparing data for analysis, including acquiring data from various sources and cleaning and preprocessing the data
- Exploring and analysing data to identify trends, patterns, and relationships
- Using dashboards, reports, and visualisations to communicate findings and recommendations to stakeholders
- Collaborating with data scientists and other stakeholders to understand their data needs and requirements
- Developing and maintaining key performance indicators and metrics to track the performance of the business
- Staying up-to-date on industry trends and best practices in business intelligence and continually learning new techniques and tools

BI analysts may work in a variety of industries, including finance, healthcare, retail, and technology, and may be involved in a wide range of projects, including customer segmentation, fraud detection, and predictive modelling.

Statistician

A statistician is a professional who uses statistical techniques to collect, analyse, and interpret data. Statisticians may work in a variety of fields, including academia, government, and industry, and may be involved in a wide range of projects, including designing and analysing experiments, developing statistical models, and conducting data analyses.

Some specific tasks that a statistician may be responsible for include:

- Designing and analysing experiments and surveys to collect data
- Collecting and preparing data for analysis, including acquiring data from various sources and cleaning and preprocessing the data
- Using statistical techniques to analyse and interpret data and to test hypotheses
- Developing statistical models to solve problems and make predictions
- Communicating findings and recommendations to stakeholders through reports, presentations, and visualisations
- Collaborating with data scientists and other stakeholders to understand their data needs and requirements
- Staying up-to-date on industry trends and best practices in statistics and continually learning new techniques and tools

Statisticians may work in various industries, including finance, healthcare, retail, and technology, and may be involved in a wide range of projects, including customer segmentation, fraud detection, and predictive modelling.

Data Product Manager

A data product manager is responsible for developing and managing data-driven products and services within an organisation. This may involve working with data scientists and other team members to identify opportunities for using data to create value for customers and developing a roadmap for bringing data products to market.

- Some specific tasks that a data product manager may be responsible for include:
- Identifying and prioritising opportunities for using data to create value for customers
- Defining the target market and value proposition for data products
- Developing a roadmap for bringing data products to market
- Collaborating with data scientists and other team members to design and build data products
- Managing budgets and resources related to data product development
- Tracking and analysing the performance of data products to identify areas for improvement
- Communicating the value and capabilities of data products to customers and stakeholders

A data product manager may also be responsible for staying up-to-date on industry trends and best practices in data product development and helping educate other team members on data product management principles and techniques.

Data Manager

A data manager oversees an organisation's data assets and ensures that they are properly collected, stored, protected, and made available to authorised users. Some specific tasks that a data manager may be responsible for include:

- Developing and implementing data management policies and procedures
- Ensuring that data is collected, stored, and protected per relevant regulations and policies

- Overseeing the design and maintenance of data storage systems, including databases, data lakes, and data warehouses
- Ensuring that data is accurate and up-to-date and that data integrity is maintained
- Managing budgets and resources related to data management
- Providing guidance and support to data scientists and other team members on data management best practices and techniques
- Staying up-to-date on industry trends and best practices in data management

Data managers may work in various industries, including finance, healthcare, retail, and technology. They may be involved in a wide range of projects, including data warehousing, data lake implementation, and data pipeline development.

Data Modeller

A data modeller is a professional who designs and builds data models to support the storage and analysis of data within an organisation. Some specific responsibilities of a data modeller may include the following:

- Designing and building data models that accurately and efficiently represent the relationships between different data elements
- Working with data architects and other stakeholders to understand their data needs and requirements and developing data models to meet those needs
- Ensuring that data models are scalable, flexible, and maintainable
- Validating and testing data models to ensure that they are accurate and meet the needs of the organisation

- Documenting data models and their properties, including definitions of data elements, relationships, and rules
- Collaborating with data scientists and other team members to understand their data needs and requirements
- Staying up-to-date on industry trends and best practices in data modelling and continually learning new techniques and tools

Data modellers may work in various industries, including finance, healthcare, retail, and technology. They may be involved in many projects, including data warehousing, data lake implementation, and data pipeline development.

Director of Data Science

The responsibilities of a director of data science may vary depending on the specific organisation and industry, but some typical duties may include the following:

- Leading and managing a team of data scientists and other data professionals
- Setting the overall strategy and vision for the data science function within the organisation
- Collaborating with stakeholders across the organisation to understand their data needs and requirements and developing data-driven solutions to meet those needs
- Overseeing the development and implementation of data-driven projects and initiatives
- Ensuring that data governance and privacy policies are in place and followed
- Managing budgets and resources related to data science projects and initiatives

- Staying up-to-date on industry trends and best practices in data science and continually learning new
  techniques and tools
- Communicating the value and capabilities of data science to stakeholders within the organisation

A director of data science may work in various industries, including finance, healthcare, retail, and technology, and may be involved in multiple projects, including predictive modelling, customer segmentation, fraud detection, and more.

Application Architect

An application architect is responsible for designing and implementing the technical infrastructure of an application. This includes defining the overall architecture of the application, as well as the specific components and technologies that will be used to build it.

Some specific responsibilities of an application architect may include the following:

- Designing the overall architecture of an application,
  including the technical components and how they will
  fit together
- Selecting appropriate technologies and tools for the
  application based on the needs of the business and the
  requirements of the project
- Collaborating with developers and other team members to ensure that the application is developed per the
  architecture
- Providing guidance and direction to developers on
  technical issues and best practices
- Monitoring the performance of the application and
  identifying opportunities for improvement
- Staying up-to-date with emerging technologies and
  trends in the field

Application architects typically work in various industries, including software development, finance, healthcare, and retail. They may work for a software development company, a consulting company, or in-house at a business or organisation.

Market Research Analyst

A market research analyst is responsible for gathering, analyzing, and interpreting data related to a particular market or industry. They use this data to understand trends, identify opportunities and threats, and make business and organisation recommendations.

Some specific responsibilities of a market research analyst may include the following:

- Designing and conducting surveys or focus groups to gather data
- Analysing data using statistical software or other tools
- Interpreting data and identifying trends or patterns
- Preparing reports or presentations to communicate findings to stakeholders
- Making recommendations to businesses or organisations based on data analysis
- Staying up-to-date on industry trends and developments

Market research analysts typically work in various industries, including marketing, finance, healthcare, and retail. They may work for a market research company, a consulting company, or in-house at a business or organisation.

Chief Data Officer (CDO)

The chief data officer (CDO) is a senior executive responsible for overseeing an organisation's data assets and ensuring that they are properly collected, stored, protected, and made available to authorised users. Some specific responsibilities of a CDO may include the following:

- Developing and implementing a data strategy that aligns with the overall business strategy and goals of the organisation
- Ensuring that data governance and privacy policies are in place and followed
- Overseeing the design and maintenance of data storage systems, including databases, data lakes, and data warehouses
- Ensuring that data is accurate and up-to-date and that data integrity is maintained
- Leading and managing a team of data professionals, including data scientists, data engineers, and data analysts
- Collaborating with stakeholders across the organisation to understand their data needs and requirements and developing data-driven solutions to meet those needs
- Managing budgets and resources related to data management and data-driven initiatives
- Communicating the value and capabilities of data science to stakeholders within the organisation

The CDO may also be responsible for working with senior leadership to identify and prioritise data-driven initiatives and tracking and measuring the impact of those initiatives on the business.

Data science career path

There is no specific role that you need to start in before becoming a data scientist. However, having a strong foundation in math and statistics and programming and data analysis skills is generally helpful to succeed in a data science role. Some individuals may choose to start their careers in entry-level positions such as data analyst or data engineer. In contrast, others may start as interns or in other roles that provide exposure to data and data analysis.

The Data Science Career Path

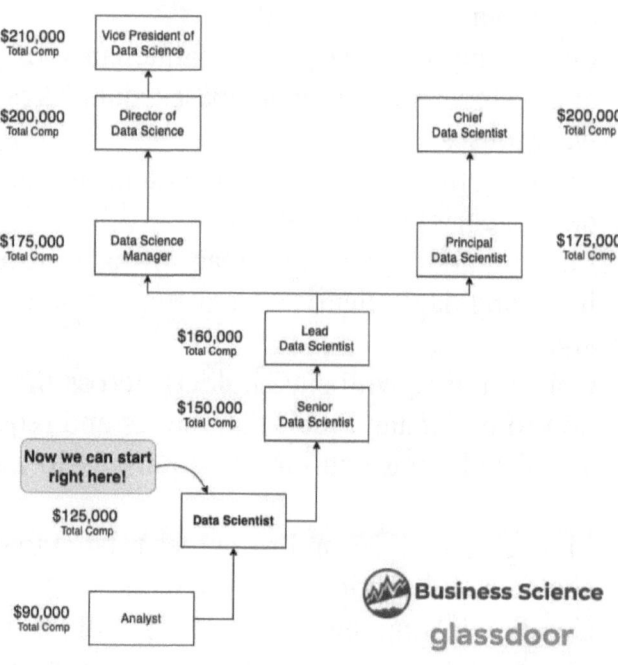

Figure 24 - Data science career guide by Glassdoor

Ultimately, the path to becoming a data scientist will depend on your education, skills, interests, and goals. It is essential to continuously learn and expand your skills and knowledge in data science and related fields and seek opportunities to gain practical experience and build expertise. Networking and building relationships with professionals in the area can also help build a successful career in data science.

Technical skills required for data science

Data science involves a wide range of technical skills, including:

Programming: Data scientists often use programming languages like Python, R, and SQL to clean, analyse, and visualise data. Familiarity with these languages is essential for data scientists.

Statistics and machine learning: Data scientists use statistical techniques and machine learning algorithms to analyse and make predictions from data. A strong understanding of these concepts is necessary for data scientists.

Data visualisation: Data scientists use tools like Tableau and Matplotlib to create visualisations of data that help communicate findings and insights to stakeholders.

Data wrangling: Data scientists often work with large and complex datasets that may be incomplete or messy. They use data cleaning and transformation techniques to prepare data for analysis.

Data storage and retrieval: Data scientists need to know how to store and retrieve data from various sources, including databases, flat files, and data lakes.

Domain expertise: Data scientists often work in specific industries or domains, such as finance, healthcare, or retail. Having a deep understanding of the industry or domain in which they are working is important for data scientists to be able to extract meaningful insights from the data.

Tools skills required for data science

Many software skills can be helpful for data scientists, including:

Programming languages: Data scientists often use Python, R, and SQL to clean, analyse, and visualise data. Familiarity with these languages is essential for data scientists.

Data visualisation tools: Tools like Tableau, Matplotlib, and D3.js are commonly used by data scientists to create data visualisations.

Data storage and retrieval tools: Data scientists may use tools like SQL, NoSQL databases, and data lakes to store and retrieve data.

Machine learning libraries: Data scientists may use machine learning libraries like scikit-learn, TensorFlow, and Keras to build and train machine learning models.

Data wrangling and transformation tools: Data scientists may use tools like Pandas and OpenRefine to clean and transform data for analysis.

Collaboration and version control tools: Data scientists often work in teams and may use tools like Git and Jupyter notebooks to collaborate and track changes to their work.

It's important to note that data science is a rapidly evolving field, and new tools and technologies are constantly emerging. Data scientists should be willing to learn and adapt to new technologies as needed continuously.

Soft skills required for data science

In addition to technical skills, a number of soft skills are important for data scientists to possess to be successful in their roles. Some of the key soft skills that are valuable for data scientists to have include:

Communication skills: Data scientists need to effectively communicate their findings and recommendations to stakeholders who may not have a technical background. This includes presenting data and analysis in a clear, concise, and understandable way, as well as writing technical reports and documents.

Collaboration skills: Data scientists often work as part of a team and need to be able to collaborate with others in order to achieve common goals effectively. This includes being able to work well with people from different disciplines and backgrounds and being able to communicate and share ideas with team members effectively.

Problem-solving skills: Data scientists need to be able to identify and solve complex problems using data and analysis. This requires the ability to think critically and creatively and to approach problems logically and systematically.

Time management skills: Data scientists may work on multiple projects simultaneously and need to manage their time effectively to meet deadlines and deliverables. This includes the ability to prioritise tasks and manage one's workload effectively.

Adaptability: The field of data science is constantly evolving, and data scientists need to adapt to new technologies and techniques as they emerge. This requires the ability to learn quickly and to be open to new ideas and approaches.

Steps to take to build a career in data science

There are a few key steps you can take to build a career in data science:

Build your skills and knowledge: Continuously learn and expand your skills and knowledge in data science and related fields, such as programming, statistics, and machine learning. Consider taking courses, earning certifications, and participating in online learning opportunities to stay up-to-date on industry trends and best practices.

Gain a strong foundation in math and statistics: Data science involves the use of statistical and mathematical techniques to analyse and interpret data, so it is important to have a strong foundation in these subjects. Consider taking courses or earning a degree in a related field such as mathematics, statistics, or computer science.

Gain practical experience: Consider working on projects on your own or as part of a team, and seek out internships or entry-level positions to gain practical experience in data science.

Learn programming and data analysis tools: Data scientists often use programming languages such as Python and R to manipulate and analyse data and tools such as SQL for working with databases. Consider taking courses or earning certifications in these tools to build your skills and knowledge.

Seek out internships or entry-level positions: Consider interning or working in entry-level positions to gain practical experience and build your skills and knowledge.

Build a portfolio of projects: One of the best ways to demonstrate your skills and capabilities as a data scientist is to build a portfolio of projects that showcase your abilities. Consider working on projects on your own or as part of a team, and be sure to document your work and share it with others.

Network and seek out opportunities: Networking is an important part of building a career in any field, and data science is no exception. Consider joining industry groups or associations, attending conferences and meetups, and seeking out internships or other opportunities to gain experience and build your network.

Stay up-to-date on industry trends and best practices: The field of data science is constantly evolving, so it is important to stay up-to-date on new techniques, tools, and best practices. Consider subscribing to industry publications, attending conferences and workshops, and participating in online learning opportunities to keep your skills and knowledge current.

Pursue advanced education: Consider earning a master's or PhD in a related field to deepen your expertise further and broaden your career opportunities.

Specialise in a particular area: Consider specialising in a particular area or application of data science, such as machine learning, natural language processing, or data visualisation, to differentiate yourself and build your expertise.

Popular data science courses

- Data Scientist Associate Certification
- IBM Certified Data Architect – Big Data
- Oracle Business Intelligence Foundation Suite 11g Certified Implementation Specialist
- SAS Certified Big Data Professional
- EMC Data Scientist - Advanced Analytics Specialist (EMCDS)
- Certification of Professional Achievement in Data Sciences
- Certification in Business Analytics
- Certificate in Analytics and Information Management
- Data Mining and Applications Graduate Certification
- Biomedical Data Science Graduate Certification

Top data scientist recruiters

Demand for data scientists is very high, and even government organisations are also warming up to the fact that Data Science is the future. Some of the top companies in India that hire Data Scientists in large numbers are:

- Amazon
- Deloitte
- Fractal Analytics
- LinkedIn
- MuSigma
- Flipkart
- IBM
- Accenture
- Citrix
- Myntra
- Dexlock
- Rudder Analytics

Data Science Life-cycle

The life cycle of data science refers to the various stages involved in using data to solve problems and make informed decisions. There are countless interpretations of the life cycle (and what data science even represents). My interpretation of this book is based on my understanding through my research and experience. However, suppose you have already covered the previous parts of this book. In that case, you will be very comfortable with this section, as it will reiterate some of the key points mentioned earlier, especially in data science methods and frameworks.

Figure 25 - Data science lifecycle

Problem identification

Problem identification in data science refers to the process of identifying a specific problem or opportunity that can be addressed through the use of data and analysis. This is the first step in the data science process, and it is critical to ensure that the problem is clearly defined and understood before proceeding to the next steps.

Some examples of problems that data scientists may identify and seek to solve include the following:

- Improving the efficiency of a business process
- Identifying patterns or trends in customer behaviour
- Predicting future outcomes or events
- Detecting anomalies or fraud
- Developing personalised recommendations or experiences for customers

In order to identify a problem, data scientists may consult with stakeholders and subject matter experts, review existing data and business processes, and consider the business goals and objectives. Once a problem has been identified, data scientists can develop a plan for collecting and analysing the data needed to address the problem.

Understanding the business

Understanding the business life cycle of data science refers to understanding how data science projects fit into a business's overall workflow and goals. This includes understanding the various stages of a data science project, from problem definition and data collection to analysis and implementation.

- Detect data touchpoints concerning business processes.
- Learn about the sources of the data, how it is handled, the decisions being made, the storage locations, and the downstream flow of the data.
- Conduct a thorough examination of the business implications of the data being used and the knowledge provided in the current system in the form of rules
- Investigate whether it is appropriate to use additional, reputable external data sources that can improve the decision boundaries.
- Check for late-arriving labels as well as the availability of the target label.

Remember, data science allows businesses to measure performance through data collection to make more educated decisions across the organisation using trends and empirical evidence to help them come up with solutions. Hence, data science answers five types of questions:

- How much? (Regression)
- What category? (Classification)
- What a group? (Clustering)
- Is this strange? (anomaly detection)
- Which option should you choose? (recommendation)

Collect and prepare data

The next step is to collect and prepare the data that will be used to solve the problem. This involves identifying the data sources that will be used and accessing and extracting the data from these sources. This may involve acquiring data from various sources, cleaning and preprocessing the data, and selecting relevant features.

There are several steps involved in the data collection process:

Identify data sources: Data scientists identify the data sources that will be used for the project. This may include internal sources, such as databases or system logs, or external sources, such as public data sets or APIs.

Access and extract data: Data scientists then access and extract the data from the identified sources. This may involve using tools like SQL or web scraping to extract data from databases or APIs or manually collecting data from sources like surveys or focus groups.

Clean and transform data: After collecting the data, data scientists may need to clean and transform the data to make it ready for analysis. This may involve tasks such as filling in missing values, correcting errors, and combining data from multiple sources.

Store and organise data: Finally, data scientists store and organise the data in a way that makes it easy to access and analyse. This may involve using tools like data lakes or databases to store the data.

It's important to note that the data collection process is ongoing, as data scientists may need to collect and update data as the project progresses continually.

Data Processing

Data processing in the data science lifecycle refers to the steps taken to prepare data for analysis. This can include cleaning, transforming, and organising data to make it ready for analysis and visualisation.

Some specific tasks that may be involved in data processing include:

Data cleaning: Data cleaning involves identifying and correcting errors or inconsistencies in the data. This may include tasks such as filling in missing values, identifying and removing duplicates, and correcting errors or inconsistencies in the data.

Data transformation: Data transformation involves changing the format or structure of the data to make it more suitable for analysis. This may include tasks such as aggregating data, pivoting data, or categorical encoding variables.

Data organisation: Data organisation involves storing and organising the data to make it easy to access and analyse. This may involve using tools like data lakes or databases to store the data.

Data processing is essential in the data science lifecycle, ensuring the data is ready for analysis and visualisation. Data scientists must have a strong understanding of data processing techniques and tools to prepare data effectively for analysis.

Data Analysis

In the data science lifecycle, data analysis refers to using statistical techniques and machine learning algorithms to extract insights and find patterns in data. This involves using tools and techniques like data visualisation, hypothesis testing, and machine learning to analyse and interpret the data.

Some specific tasks that may be involved in data analysis include:

Data exploration: Data exploration involves getting to know the data by summarising its main characteristics and identifying patterns and trends. This may involve visualising the data and using statistical techniques to identify patterns and trends.

Hypothesis testing: Hypothesis testing involves formulating and testing hypotheses about the relationships between different variables in the data. This may include using statistical tests to determine whether there is a significant relationship between the variables.

Machine learning: Machine learning involves using algorithms to learn patterns in data and make predictions or decisions automatically. Data scientists may use machine learning techniques to build models that predict outcomes or make decisions based on the data.

Data analysis is essential in the data science lifecycle, as it helps data scientists extract insights and understand the data. Data scientists need to have a strong understanding of data analysis techniques and tools to be able to analyse and interpret data effectively.

Data Modelling

Data modelling refers to the process of creating a representation or model of a real-world system or process of user data. This model is used to understand, predict, and make decisions about the system or process.

There are several types of data models, including:

Conceptual data models: These models represent the high-level concepts and relationships in a system or process without specifying the specific data structures or attributes.

Logical data models: These models represent the data structures and relationships in a system or process in a more detailed way but do not specify how the data will be physically stored.

Physical data models: These models represent the specific data structures and attributes that will be used to store and access data in a database or other data storage system.

Data modelling is an important step in the data science lifecycle, as it helps data scientists understand the relationships and dependencies between different elements in a system or process. Data scientists need to have a strong understanding of data modelling concepts and techniques to be able to represent real-world systems and processes using data effectively.

Data Visualisation

In the data science lifecycle, data visualisation refers to creating charts, graphs, and other visual representations of data to communicate findings and insights. Data visualisation is an important step in the data science process, as it helps data scientists communicate their findings to stakeholders clearly and concisely.

Some specific tasks that may be involved in data visualisation include:

Selecting appropriate visualisation tools and techniques: Data scientists may use tools like Tableau, Matplotlib, or D3.js to create data visualisations. They must select the appropriate tools and techniques based on the data and the message they want to convey.

Preparing the data for visualisation: Before creating visualisations, data scientists may need to prepare the data by aggregating, pivoting, or filtering it as needed.

Creating visualisations: Data scientists use tools and techniques to create visualisations of the data. This may involve creating charts, graphs, maps, or other types of visualisations.

Interpreting visualisations: Data scientists interpret the visualisations to extract insights and understand the data. They may also use visualisations to communicate their findings to stakeholders.

Data scientists need to have a strong understanding of data visualisation concepts and techniques to be able to communicate their findings and insights using visualisations effectively. We will see more about this later.

Business Value Creation

In the data science lifecycle, business value creation refers to the process of using data and data science techniques to create value for a business or organisation. This may involve using data to improve decision-making, optimise business processes, or create new products or services.

Some specific ways that data science can create business value include:

Improving decision-making: Data science can help businesses make better decisions by providing insights and predictions based on data analysis.

Optimising business processes: Data science can be used to identify inefficiencies and optimise business processes, such as supply chain management or customer service.

Creating new products or services: Data science can be used to identify new opportunities and create innovative products or services based on data-driven insights.

Reducing costs: Data science can identify cost-saving opportunities and optimise resource allocation, resulting in reduced costs for the business.

Business value creation is an important aspect of data science, as it helps businesses and organisations use data to drive growth and improve operations.

Data scientists need to understand the business context in which their work is being conducted and to align their efforts with the overall goals and objectives of the organisation.

Data Science Models

In data science, a model represents or approximates a real-world system or process user data. Models are used to understand, predict, and make decisions about the system or process.

Data Science models exist in a variety of flavours and use diverse methodologies; fortunately, the most sophisticated models are built on a few foundations.

Suppose you want to construct a predictive model. In that case, it may seem as though only cutting-edge methods will be able to address all of your issues as you get sucked into the Machine Learning and Artificial Intelligence hype vortex. However, as you become more familiar with the code, you realise that the reality is very different. Many of the issues you will encounter as a data scientist are resolved by combining several other models, most of which have been around for a very long time. Let's look at different models:

Linear regression

Linear regression is a statistical method used to model the relationship between a dependent variable and one or more independent variables. It is used to predict the dependent variable's value based on the independent variables' values.

Linear regression assumes that the relationship between the dependent variable and the independent variables is linear, which means that the change in the dependent variable is proportional to the change in the independent variables. A linear equation of the form represents this:

$$y = a + bx1 + cx2 +$$

Where y is the dependent variable, x1, x2, etc. are the independent variables, and a, b, c, etc. are the model's coefficients.

The coefficients represent the effect of each independent variable on the dependent variable.

To build a linear regression model, data scientists collect data on the dependent and independent variables and use statistical techniques to estimate the model's coefficients. They can then use the model to make predictions about the dependent variable based on new values of the independent variables.

Linear regression

Logistic regression is a statistical method used to model the probability of a binary outcome, such as the likelihood of an event occurring or the likelihood of an individual belonging to a particular group. It is used to predict the probability that an event will occur (e.g. the probability that a customer will purchase a product) or the probability that an individual belongs to a particular group (e.g. the probability that a patient has a particular disease).

Logistic regression models the probability of a binary outcome as a function of one or more independent variables. A logistic function of the form represents this:

$$p = 1 / (1 + e^{\wedge}(-z))$$

Where p is the probability of the event occurring, z is a linear combination of the independent variables, and e is the base of the natural logarithm.

To build a logistic regression model, data scientists collect data on the dependent variable (the binary outcome) and the independent variables and use statistical techniques to estimate the model's coefficients. They can then use the model to predict the probability of the event occurring or the probability that an individual belongs to a particular group based on the values of the independent variables.

Decision tree

A decision tree is a tree-like model used to make decisions or predictions based on a set of conditions. It is a machine learning algorithm to classify or predict outcomes based on features or attributes.

A decision tree consists of a series of nodes, with each node representing a decision or a condition. The tree is constructed by splitting the data into groups based on the values of the features or attributes. The resulting groups are called branches, and the endpoints of the branches are called leaves.

To build a decision tree, data scientists start at the root node and split the data into groups based on the values of a feature or attribute. They then split the data into smaller groups at each subsequent node until the leaves are pure, containing only one class or outcome.

Decision trees help make predictions or decisions in a wide range of applications, including classification tasks, fraud detection, and medical diagnosis. They are easy to understand and interpret and can handle numerical and categorical data. However, they can be prone to overfitting, so they may not generalise well to new data.

Logistic regression is a widely used statistical technique particularly useful for modelling binary outcomes and making predictions in classification tasks. It is also used in medical research and marketing to predict customer behaviour.

Random forest

Random forest is a machine learning algorithm for classification, regression, and other tasks. It is an ensemble method which combines the predictions of multiple decision trees to make a final prediction.

A random forest consists of a collection of decision trees, each of which is trained on a random sample of the data. The final prediction is made by aggregating the predictions of the individual trees, such as by taking the average or the majority vote.

To build a random forest, data scientists split the data into training and test sets. They then train multiple decision trees on the training set using a random sample of the data. The test set is used to evaluate the performance of the random forest.

Random forests are useful for making predictions or decisions in a wide range of applications, including classification, regression, and feature selection. They effectively reduce overfitting, which means they tend to generalise well to new data.

They are also resistant to noise and outliers in the data and can handle both numerical and categorical data. However, they can be more computationally expensive than other machine learning algorithms.

XGBoost/LightGBM

XGBoost (eXtreme Gradient Boosting) and LightGBM (Light Gradient Boosting Machine) are two popular gradient boosting algorithms used for classification, regression, and other tasks. They are both tree-based algorithms that build a model by training a series of decision trees, with each tree being trained to correct the mistakes made by the previous tree.

XGBoost and LightGBM are both implementations of gradient boosting that have been optimised for efficiency and performance. They both use tree ensembles, with each tree being trained on a different subset of the data. They also both use a variant of the gradient descent algorithm to optimise the model parameters.

XGBoost and LightGBM are both widely used in machine learning competitions and have been successful in a number of real-world applications. They are often used in conjunction with other machine learning algorithms and techniques, such as feature engineering and hyperparameter tuning, to improve their performance.

Artificial Neural Networks

Artificial neural networks (ANNs) are machine learning algorithms inspired by the human brain's structure and function. They are used for classification, regression, and pattern recognition tasks.

An ANN consists of a series of interconnected nodes, or neurons, that are organised into layers. Each neuron in the network receives input from the neurons in the previous layer, processes it, and passes it on to the neurons in the next layer. The input layer receives input data, and the output layer produces the output of the network. The layers in between are called hidden layers.

To train an ANN, data scientists feed it a large amount of data and adjust the weights of the connections between the neurons to minimise the error between the predicted output and the true output. This process is known as training the network and is typically done using a variant of the gradient descent algorithm.

ANNs are powerful machine learning algorithms that can learn and adapt to complex patterns in data. They are widely used in a variety of applications, including image and speech recognition, natural language processing, and financial forecasting. However, they can be computationally expensive and require a large amount of data to train effectively.

These models should give you an excellent head start in Data Science and Machine Learning. By learning them, you will be prepared to learn more advanced models and easily grasp the math behind those models.

Data Science Business Strategy

It's crucial to fully comprehend the management of your data life cycle and the upkeep of the company data model. To create the best working strategy with the organisation, you must comprehend the data that it possesses. It will then be useful for business. A roadmap for building a platform for data science is being built and improved concurrently with the initial pilots. This roadmap includes developing the storage platform and methods for working with machine learning models.

Define the business objectives: Identify the specific business goals that data science can help achieve, such as improving customer satisfaction, increasing efficiency, or reducing costs.

Assess the current data landscape: Identify the data sources and systems currently being used and any data gaps or challenges. Determine what data is needed to support the business objectives.

Identify potential data science projects: Identify specific data science projects that can help achieve the business objectives, such as predicting customer churn, optimising marketing campaigns, or improving supply chain efficiency.

Prioritise projects: Determine which projects should be prioritised based on their potential impact and the resources required to complete them.

Develop a plan: Create a detailed plan for implementing the data science projects, including timelines, budgets, and resources.

Communicate the strategy: Communicate the data science business strategy to stakeholders, including the business objectives, the specific projects that will be undertaken, and the expected outcomes.

By following these steps, you can create a data science business strategy aligned with the organisation's goals and leverage the power of data science to create value.

Creating a vision

A compelling vision unites all parties to a common goal, inspires change, and encourages action. Without one, you'll probably become mired in the details of the day-to-day difficulties and excessively concentrate on immediate chances.

Create a compelling vision as a result. The finest ones adhere to the organisation's objective, concentrate on fruitful consequences, and avoid business or technical jargon. The why, how, and what of your organisation's data science approach can be further defined by supporting artefacts like mission statements, value statements, and philosophies.

Handing cultural hurdles

The biggest obstacle for leading companies in their efforts to become data-driven remains cultural hurdles, according to a NewVantage Partners Big Data and AI 2021 Survey (92.2%).[7]

As a result, an effective data science strategic plan considers organisational and industry-specific cultural difficulties. According to the poll, the following are typical problems:

- Organisational alignment
- Business processes
- Change management
- Communication
- People skillsets
- Resistance or lack of understanding to enable change

On the plus side, an effective strategy plan evaluates the cultural factors that may support adopting data-driven decision-making. Analyse how data may help your company's beliefs and mission, as well as the personal motivations of your coworkers.

A data science club, lunch and learns, dev talks, hands-on labs, recruitment events, designated chat/support rooms, and assistance from internal communications are some specific strategies that could promote the organisation's culture.

Building an effective team

Building an effective team is essential for a company's data science strategy because data science involves a wide range of tasks, from data collection and cleaning to model training and deployment. An effective team will have the necessary skills and expertise to handle these tasks, allowing the company to maximise the value of its data and use it to make informed business decisions.

Having a solid team also allows for better collaboration and communication, leading to more efficient problem-solving and faster project turnaround. Additionally, a diverse team with different perspectives and experiences can bring a wealth of ideas and approaches to the table, leading to more innovative and effective solutions.

Overall, an effective data science team is critical to the success of a company's data science strategy and can have a significant impact on the organisation's bottom line.

Choose the right data

Over the past few years, a lot has changed in the world of data and modelling. While the opportunity to broaden insights by merging data is increasing, so is the volume of information. Companies may now see their business environment more precisely and in more detail thanks to bigger and better data. Operations, customer experiences, and strategy are all improved when it is possible to see what was previously invisible. You must therefore improve in two areas:

    1. Source data creatively

2. Get the necessary IT support

Company	Market Cap	Strong Data Strategy
Microsoft	$1.78 T	YES
Apple	$2.10 T	YES
Alphabet (Google)	$1.16 T	YES
Amazon	$869.69 B	YES
Tesla	$385.89 B	YES
Netflix	$131.27 B	YES

Table 1 - World's most valuable companies with strong data strategy

An effective data strategy will define comprehensive data governance issues such as ethical data use and how to make data FAIR[8]:

- *Findable* – Make data and metadata easy to find by both humans and machines.
- *Accessible* – Authorised and authenticated users can access the appropriate data.
- *Interoperable* – Data sets should be easily combined with other data sets and applications.
- *Reusable* – Don't reinvent the wheel by creating re-dundant data sets representing multiple sources of truth. Instead, data sets should be reused.

Build models that predict and optimise business outcomes

While data are crucial, analytics models that let managers forecast and optimise results are what lead to performance improvements and competitive advantage.

More importantly, the best model development method typically begins not with the data but rather with identifying a business opportunity and evaluating how the model may enhance performance.

As per Mckinsey, hypothesis-led modelling produces quicker results and grounds models in real-world data linkages that managers can more readily comprehend.

Transform your company's capabilities

Senior executives' top issue, which they frequently voice, is that their managers don't employ big data-based models because they don't comprehend or have confidence in them.

These issues frequently result from a mismatch between an organisation's current culture and capabilities and the newest strategies for successfully utilising analytics.

The new strategies either don't match how businesses make decisions or don't offer a clear road map for achieving corporate objectives. Tools appear to be created more for modelling experts than front-line workers. Few managers find the models compelling enough to promote their use — a critical flaw if businesses want the new methodologies to spread throughout the organisation. The bottom message is that exploiting big data requires a deliberate organisational change in three areas:

1. Develop business-relevant analytics that can be put to use
2. Embed analytics in simple tools for the front lines
3. Develop capabilities to exploit big data

Building data lake

There are several steps involved in building a data lake for data science in an organisation:

Define the purpose and scope of the data lake: The first step is to determine what data types will be stored in the data lake and how they will be used. This will help to define the architecture and design of the data lake.

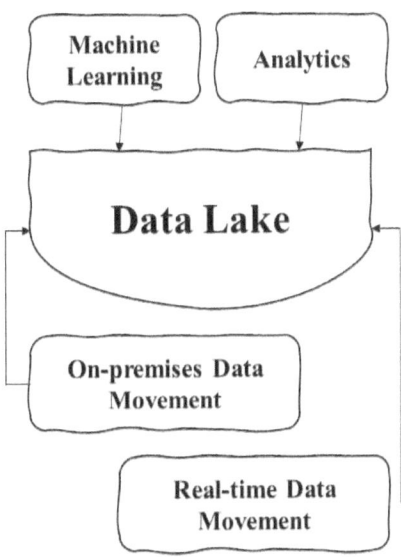

Figure 26 - A data lake is a centralised repository that allows you to store all your structured and unstructured data at any scale.

Select the appropriate technology: Several technology options are available for building a data lake, including open-source options like Apache Hadoop and commercial offerings like Amazon Web Services (AWS) and Microsoft Azure. Choosing a scalable, flexible, and cost-effective technology for the organisation is important.

Load and integrate data: The next step is to load and integrate the data into the data lake. This may involve extracting data from various sources, such as databases, applications, and sensors, and transforming it into a standardised format.

Implement security and governance: It is important to implement security and governance measures to protect the data in the data lake and ensure it is used appropriately. This may involve establishing access controls, establishing data lineage and auditing processes, and defining data retention policies.

Provide access to the data: Once the data lake is set up, it is important to provide access to the data for data scientists and other users. This may involve setting up APIs, data catalogues, or other access mechanisms to allow users to discover and query the data.

Monitor and maintain the data lake: Ongoing maintenance is important to ensure the data lake runs smoothly and meets the organisation's needs. This may involve monitoring the data lake for performance, troubleshooting issues, and updating and upgrading as needed.

Business intelligence

Business intelligence (BI) is a set of technologies, processes, and practices that are used to transform raw data into actionable insights and knowledge that can inform business decisions. BI systems typically involve the following components:

Data sources: BI systems draw data from various sources, such as transactional databases, spreadsheets, log files, and external data sources.

Data integration and management: BI systems consolidate and clean data from multiple sources and store it in a central repository or data warehouse.

Data analysis and visualisation: BI systems provide tools and techniques for analysing and visualising data, such as pivot tables, charts, and dashboards. These tools allow users to explore and analyse data, identify trends and patterns, and gain insights into business performance.

Reporting and delivery: BI systems provide mechanisms for distributing reports and dashboards to stakeholders, such as business executives, managers, and analysts.

BI systems can be used in various applications, including sales and marketing, finance, operations, and human resources. They can help organisations to make data-driven decisions, improve efficiency, and gain a competitive advantage.

Business Intelligence & Data Science

Business intelligence (BI) and data science are related but distinct fields that involve the use of data to inform decision-making and improve business operations.

Business intelligence is focused on using data to support an organisation's strategic and tactical decision-making. It involves using tools and techniques to collect, store, and analyse data from internal and external sources and to present the results of this analysis in a meaningful and actionable way for business stakeholders.

On the other hand, data science is a broader field that encompasses a range of techniques and approaches for extracting insights and knowledge from data. It involves using statistical and machine learning techniques to analyse and interpret data and applying these techniques to solve problems and inform decision-making.

In practice, there is often overlap between the two fields, with business intelligence tools and techniques used to support data science projects and data science techniques used to inform business decision-making.

However, the focus and goals of the two fields are slightly different, with business intelligence being more closely aligned with the needs of the business and data science being more focused on using data to extract insights and solve problems.

Data Science Project Management

As the volume of data increases day by day in all areas and industries, it is essential for any company, industry, or domain to know about it and use it appropriately to grow enormously. No business wants to slow down growth, and then they do not see the root of the problem and how to solve it and develop it. Often when we talk about data science projects, it seems that no one can explain how the whole process is going. From data collection to analysis and presentation of results. In the previous section, we saw the data science lifecycle, and now we will apply them in the data science project

Problem statement

The problem statement-based data science technique has two options: explore the issue and find a solution. You must first decide if a numerical or categorical choice is your primary objective in using this data. Your problem statement might be, for instance, if a drug has produced the anticipated outcomes, whether customers are happy with a newly released product, or whether sales will increase or decrease in the future. This is a definitive response, meaning it is either yes or no, or perhaps. Imagine your job is forecasting future sales, property values, or the recommended dosage. Based on the given information, they all provide numerical values. Therefore, you must first identify the issue and choose the appropriate remedy.

Understanding data or business

Understanding the terminology and having expertise in the field of understanding will help us develop better solutions because the problem might occur in various regions or areas. As a result, we gain knowledge of several additional proposals that are solely based on our existing understanding of the local business environment.

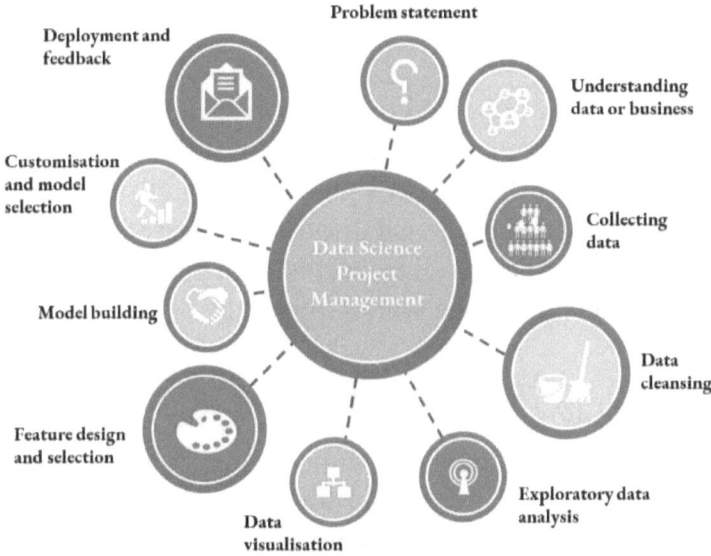

Figure 27 - Data science project deliverables

Collecting data

The data is now collected from numerous sources and placed in a designated area as the data processing process begins (database). The information needed to remedy this issue has been gathered.

Data cleansing

The loaded data is correctly examined for abnormalities, missing data, and distribution. Together with all of the payloads, the data is cleaned and processed.

Exploratory data analysis

As all data is cleared, and the necessary part is removed, leaving unnecessary things. The data is now analysed and studied along with all statistics.

Data visualisation

Since most of the collected data is now cleaned up, explored and well understood and presented visually with graphs, graphs using the Scikit-learn library in Python or visualisation can be created in Tableau and some visualisation software in something else. In this way, ideas are well extracted with perfect images that anyone can see which can be well explained.

Feature design and selection

Implement some statistical or dimensionality reduction techniques or other techniques, as appropriate, to add valuable columns from existing or new columns and provide only the data you need here and not any others. Otherwise, there is a possibility of misinterpretation.

Model building

During the model-building phase, the data is split into two parts, one of which is used for training and the other for validation because if you use the same data, there is a chance that the machine will be overfitted (instead of studying the data, ideally studying the subject or data theory).

Machine learning comes in different types and is used differently, depending on the data and requirements. Styles include supervised, unsupervised, and reinforcement learning. So, the required models are implemented, and the best model is selected. We will go into more details later.

Customisation and model selection

We do not know which model is the suitable one to choose from. So, after building the model, they are evaluated and additionally adjusted with some other parameters, and then a model is selected that has proven itself well.

Figure 28 - Data science technology stack

Deployment and Feedback

The required machine-learning algorithm has been selected and is now deployed. Once deployed, it is used by a company or customers and feedback is collected; if it works well, the problem is resolved; otherwise, it will be retrieved by the data analysis team again for further improvements, so this will be done by re-checking. This can be done in many different ways, and there are many tools, like Flask, AWS, Google Cloud, Django etc.

Statistical Concepts of Data Science

Statistics study involves gathering, analysing, interpreting, and presenting vast amounts of numerical data. If you add programming and machine learning to the mix, you can accurately describe data science's fundamental skills. Nearly every aspect of data science uses statistics. It is utilised for data analysis, transformation, and cleanup. Analysis and improvement of machine learning methods. Additionally, ideas and insights are presented using it.

Given the breadth of the statistics area, it might be difficult to pinpoint precisely what you must learn and in what order. Additionally, many of this subject's learning materials are complicated. Sometimes it can be challenging to understand, especially if you don't have a degree in advanced mathematics and are switching from a career like software engineering to data science. So, as it is just a beginner's guide, I will keep this very simple.

Statistical sample

In data science, a statistical sample is a subset of a population that is selected for analysis. The goal of sampling is to conclude the population based on the characteristics of the sample. Sampling allows data scientists to work with a smaller, more manageable dataset rather than trying to analyse the entire population.

There are several different types of sampling techniques that can be used in data science, including:

Simple random sampling: This involves selecting a sample from the population using a random process, such as drawing names out of a hat.

Stratified sampling: This involves dividing the population into subgroups (strata) and then selecting a sample from each subgroup. This technique is used when the population is heterogeneous, and it is important to ensure that the sample is representative of each subgroup.

Cluster sampling: This involves dividing the population into clusters and then selecting a sample of clusters for analysis. This technique is often used when it is difficult or impractical to sample individuals from the entire population.

Systematic sampling: This involves selecting a sample from the population by selecting every nth member of the population, where n is determined based on the size of the population and the desired sample size.

It is important to carefully design the sampling process in order to ensure that the sample is representative of the population and that the conclusions drawn from the sample are accurate.

Descriptive statistics

Descriptive statistics is a set of statistical techniques used to summarise, organise, and describe data. The goal of descriptive statistics is to provide a concise summary of the main characteristics of a dataset, such as its central tendency, dispersion, and distribution.

Some common descriptive statistics used in data science include:

Mean: The mean measures central tendency representing a dataset's average value. It is calculated by adding up all the values in the dataset and dividing them by the number of values.

Median: The median is another measure of central tendency representing a dataset's median value. It is calculated by arranging the values in the dataset in numerical order and selecting the middle value.

Mode: The mode is the value that occurs most frequently in a dataset.

Range: The range is a measure of dispersion representing the difference between a dataset's highest and lowest values.

Variance: The variance is a measure of dispersion that represents how spread out the values in a dataset is. It is calculated by taking the sum of the squared differences between each value and the mean and dividing it by the number of values.

Standard deviation: The standard deviation is a measure of dispersion representing the average distance of the values in a dataset from the mean. It is calculated by taking the square root of the variance.

Percentiles: Percentiles divide a dataset into 100 equal parts and are used to identify the value at a specific point in the distribution. For example, the 50th percentile is the value greater than or equal to 50% of the values in the dataset.

Descriptive statistics are a valuable tool for understanding and summarising data, and they are often used as a starting point for more advanced statistical analysis.

Probability

Probability is a measure of the likelihood of an event occurring. In data science, probability is used to model and analyse uncertain events, such as the outcome of a coin toss or the success of a marketing campaign.

Probability is usually expressed as a decimal or fraction between 0 and 1, where 0 represents an impossible event, and 1 represents a certain event. For example, the probability of flipping a coin and getting heads is 0.5, or 50%.

Several types of probability are important in data science:

Marginal probability: Marginal probability refers to the probability of a single event occurring. For example, the probability of flipping a coin and getting heads is 0.5.

Joint probability: Joint probability refers to the probability of two events occurring simultaneously. For example, the probability of flipping a coin and getting heads and rolling a dice and getting a 4 is 0.5 x (1/6) = 0.0833, or 8.33%.

Conditional probability: Conditional probability refers to the probability of an event occurring given that another event has already occurred. For example, the probability of flipping a coin and getting heads, given that the coin is fair, is 0.5, while the probability of flipping a coin and getting heads, given that the coin is biased, is not 0.5.

Independence: Independence refers to the idea that the probability of an event occurring is not affected by the occurrence of other events. For example, the probability of flipping a coin and getting heads is independent of the probability of rolling a dice and getting a 4.

Understanding probability is important for data science because it allows data scientists to model and analyse uncertain events and make predictions about the likelihood of different outcomes.

Bias

In data science, bias refers to the systematic error or distortion in the data collection or analysis process that leads to incorrect or incomplete conclusions. Bias can occur at any stage of the data science process, from data collection and cleaning to model training and evaluation.

There are several types of bias that can occur in data science:

Sample bias: Sample bias occurs when the sample selected for analysis is not representative of the population. This can lead to incorrect conclusions about the population based on the characteristics of the sample.

Selection bias: Selection bias occurs when the data collection process is not random, and certain groups or individuals are more likely to be included in the sample. This can lead to a biased sample that is not representative of the population.

Confirmation bias: Confirmation bias occurs when data is selectively interpreted or analysed to confirm a preconceived belief or hypothesis. This can lead to the acceptance of incorrect or incomplete conclusions.

Algorithmic bias: Algorithmic bias occurs when a machine learning algorithm is trained on biased data or is designed to introduce bias into the results. This can lead to biased outcomes or predictions.

It is important to identify and correct for bias in the data science process in order to ensure that the conclusions and predictions made from the data are accurate and unbiased.

Correlation

In data science, correlation refers to the statistical relationship between two variables. It indicates the extent to which the variables are related and whether they tend to increase or decrease together.

There are two types of correlation: positive correlation and negative correlation. A positive correlation means that the variables increase or decrease together, while a negative correlation means that one variable increases as the other decreases.

Correlation can be quantified using the Pearson correlation coefficient, which ranges from -1 to 1. A value of -1 indicates a strong negative correlation, a value of 0 indicates no correlation, and a value of 1 indicates a strong positive correlation.

Correlation is an important concept in data science because it allows data scientists to identify patterns and relationships in the data and make predictions about future outcomes. For example, if there is a strong positive correlation between the number of hours a student studies and their test scores, a data scientist might predict that a student who studies more will have a higher test score.

However, it is important to note that correlation does not imply causation. Just because two variables are correlated does not mean that one causes the other. It is important to consider other factors and conduct additional analysis to determine the true relationship between the variables.

Methods and Metrics

Many methods and metrics are used in data science for tasks such as data collection, cleaning, exploration, visualisation, modelling, and evaluation. Some common methods and metrics include:

Data collection methods: These include methods such as surveys, experiments, and web scraping, which are used to gather data from various sources.

Data cleaning methods: These include methods such as missing value imputation and outlier detection, which are used to prepare the data for analysis by removing or correcting errors and inconsistencies.

Data exploration methods: These include methods such as descriptive statistics and data visualisation, which are used to understand the characteristics and patterns in the data.

Data visualisation methods: These include methods such as bar charts, scatter plots, and histograms, which are used to visualise the data and communicate findings.

Modelling methods: These include methods such as regression, classification, and clustering, which are used to build predictive models from the data.

Evaluation metrics: These include metrics such as accuracy, precision, and recall, which are used to evaluate the performance of a model.

These are just a few examples of the many methods and metrics used in data science. The specific methods and metrics used will depend on the specific goals and needs of the project.

Confidence interval

A confidence interval is a range of values calculated from a sample of data and used to estimate a population parameter. It is called a "confidence" interval because it represents the range of values likely to contain the true population parameter with a certain confidence level.

For example, if a 95% confidence interval for the mean of a population is calculated as (10, 15), the true population mean is likely to be within the range of 10 to 15 with 95% confidence.

The sample size and the confidence level determine the confidence interval's width. A larger sample size and higher confidence level will result in a narrower confidence interval. In comparison, a smaller sample size and a lower level of confidence will result in a wider confidence interval.

Confidence intervals are used in data science to provide a range of values within which the true population parameter is likely to fall, given the sample data. They are useful for understanding estimates' precision and making decisions based on the data.

Confusion matrix

A confusion matrix is a table used to evaluate a classification model's performance. It is called a "confusion" matrix because it helps visualise the confusion between predicted and actual classes.

The confusion matrix is typically used to calculate several evaluation metrics, such as accuracy, precision, and recall. These metrics are calculated using the following definitions:

True Positive (TP): The number of instances where the model correctly predicted the positive class.

True Negative (TN): The number of instances where the model correctly predicted the negative class.

False Positive (FP): The number of instances where the model incorrectly predicted the positive class.

False Negative (FN): The number of instances where the model incorrectly predicted the negative class.

Using these definitions, the following evaluation metrics can be calculated:

Accuracy: The proportion of correct predictions made by the model, calculated as (TP + TN) / (TP + TN + FP + FN)

Precision: The proportion of correct positive predictions, calculated as TP / (TP + FP)

Recall: The proportion of actual positive cases that are correctly predicted, calculated as TP / (TP + FN)

		Predicted	
		Negative (N) -	Positive (P) +
Actual	Negative -	True Negative (TN)	False Positive (FP) Type I Error
	Positive +	False Negative (FN) Type II Error	True Positive (TP)

Figure 29 - Confusion matrix visualisation

A confusion matrix is useful for understanding a classification model's performance and identifying areas where the model can be improved. It is commonly used in data science to evaluate the accuracy of machine learning models.

Gain and Lift Chart

Gain and lift charts are graphical tools used to evaluate the performance of a classification model, particularly in the context of marketing and customer segmentation. They are used to visualise the expected return on investment (ROI) from using the model to target a specific group of customers.

A gain chart is a plot of the percentage of the target population (e.g. customers who will respond to a marketing campaign) against the percentage of the total population reached. The curve shows the incremental gain in response rate as the percentage of the total population increases.

A lift chart is similar to a gain chart, but it compares the model's performance to a random population selection. The curve shows the lift in response rate (i.e. the improvement over random selection) as the percentage of the total population increases.

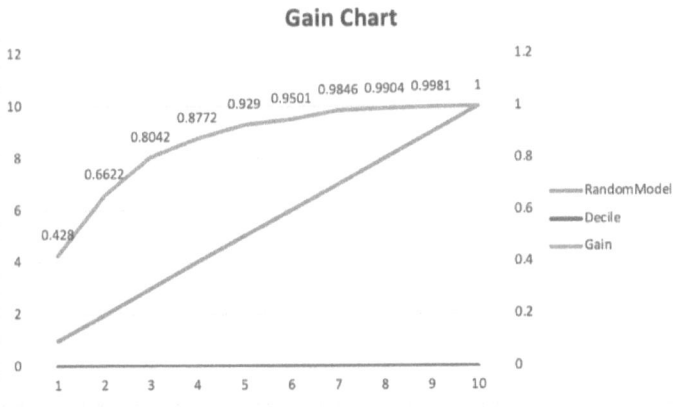

Figure 30 - A gain chart

Gain and lift charts are useful for understanding a classification model's effectiveness and identifying the optimal point at which to target a specific group of customers. They are commonly used in data science to evaluate the performance of machine learning models in marketing and customer segmentation applications.

Kolmogorov-Smirnov Chart

The Kolmogorov-Smirnov (KS) chart is a graphical tool used to evaluate the quality of a sample of data. It is based on the Kolmogorov-Smirnov test, which is a statistical test used to determine whether a sample of data comes from a known distribution.

The KS chart is a plot of the cumulative distribution function (CDF) of the sample data and the CDF of the known distribution. If the two curves are close, it suggests that the sample data is likely to come from the known distribution. If the curves are significantly different, it suggests that the sample data does not come from the known distribution.

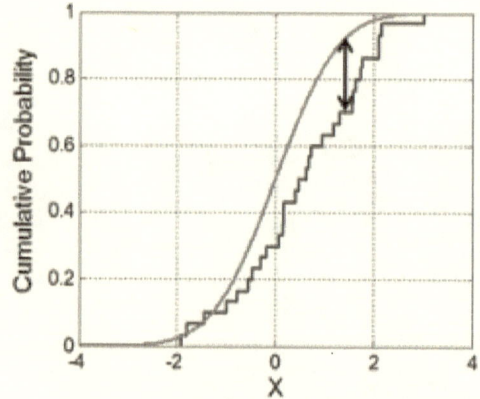

Figure 31 - Kolmogorov-Smirnov Chart

The KS chart is a useful tool for understanding the distribution of a sample of data and for identifying any deviations from a known distribution. It is commonly used in data science to evaluate the quality of a data sample and determine whether it is appropriate to use a particular statistical model or analysis technique.

Chi-Square

The chi-square test (also known as the chi-squared test or Pearson's chi-square test) is a statistical test used to determine whether there is a significant difference between the observed frequencies of a categorical variable and the expected frequencies based on a particular hypothesis.

The chi-square test is based on the chi-square statistic, calculated as the sum of the squared differences between the observed and expected frequencies divided by the expected frequencies. The larger the chi-square statistic, the greater the difference between the observed and expected frequencies and the more likely it is that the difference is not due to chance.

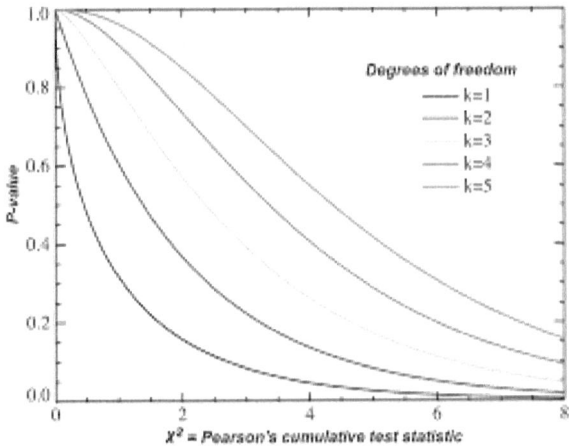

Figure 32 - Chi-square test

The chi-square test is commonly used in data science to test hypotheses about categorical data, such as whether the proportions of different categories in a sample are significantly different from the proportions in the population. It is also used to test the independence of two categorical variables.

The chi-square test is a widely used statistical tool for understanding the relationships between categorical variables and making inferences about a population based on a sample of data.

ROC curve

A receiver operating characteristic (ROC) curve is a graphical tool used to evaluate the performance of a binary classification model. It is a plot of the true positive rate (TPR) against the false positive rate (FPR) at various classification thresholds.

The true positive rate is the proportion of positive cases that are correctly predicted by the model, while the false positive rate is the proportion of negative cases that are incorrectly predicted as positive.

The ROC curve allows data scientists to visualise the trade-off between the TPR and FPR and select the model's optimal classification threshold. A model with a higher TPR and a lower FPR is considered to have a better performance.

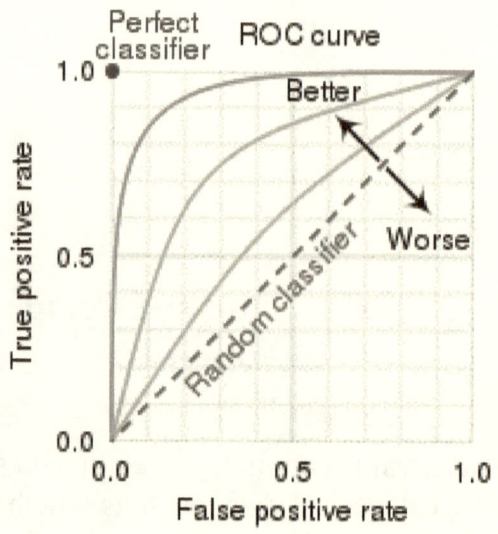

Figure 33 - A receiver operating characteristic (ROC) curve

The area under the ROC curve (AUC) is a metric used to summarise the model's performance. A model with an AUC of 1.0 is considered to have a perfect performance, while a model with an AUC of 0.5 is considered to have a random performance.

The ROC curve is a widely used tool in data science for evaluating the performance of binary classification models. It is useful for understanding the trade-off between the true positive rate and the false positive rate and for selecting the optimal classification threshold for the model.

Gini Coefficient

The Gini coefficient is a measure of statistical dispersion used to evaluate a variable's inequality or distribution. It ranges from 0 to 1, where a value of 0 indicates perfect equality (i.e. all values are the same), and a value of 1 indicates perfect inequality (i.e. one value is much larger than all the others).

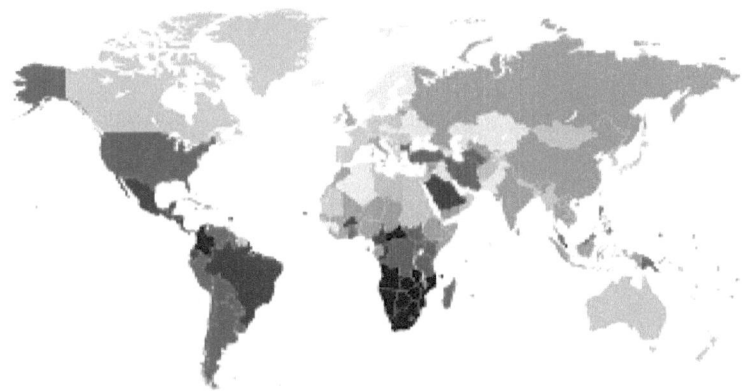

Figure 34 - Gini Coefficient

The Gini coefficient is calculated as the ratio of the sum of the absolute differences between the variable and the mean divided by the mean and the number of observations. It is often used to measure income inequality within a population or evaluate wealth distribution or other economic indicators.

In data science, the Gini coefficient is often used as an evaluation metric for decision tree models. It is used to measure the purity of the splits in the tree and to choose the split that results in the greatest reduction in Gini impurity.

The Gini coefficient is useful for understanding a variable's inequality or distribution and evaluating the decision tree models' performance.

Root Mean Square Error (RMSE)

Root Mean Square Error (RMSE) is a measure of the difference between the predicted values of a model and the true values. It is commonly used to evaluate the performance of regression models and is calculated as the square root of the mean squared error (MSE).

The MSE is calculated as the average of the squared differences between predicted and true values. The RMSE is the square root of the MSE, which is expressed in the same units as the original data.

$$RMSE = \sqrt{\sum_{i=1}^{n} \frac{(\hat{y}_i - y_i)^2}{n}}$$

Figure 35 - Mean Square Error (RMSE)

The RMSE is a widely used evaluation metric in data science because it balances the magnitude of the errors and the number of errors. It is a useful tool for understanding the overall error of a model and for comparing the performance of different models.

A model with a lower RMSE is generally considered to be more accurate and to have a better fit for the data. However, it is important to note that the RMSE is sensitive to outliers and can be influenced by the scale of the data.

The L1 version of RMSE

The L1 version of RMSE, also known as the mean absolute error (MAE), is a measure of the difference between the predicted values of a model and the true values. It is calculated as the average of the absolute differences between predicted and true values.

MAE is similar to RMSE but less sensitive to outliers because it uses the absolute values of the errors rather than the squared errors. This means that large errors do not have as much of an impact on the overall error of the model as they do in RMSE.

MAE is a commonly used evaluation metric in data science, particularly for regression models. It is a useful tool for understanding the overall error of a model and for comparing the performance of different models.

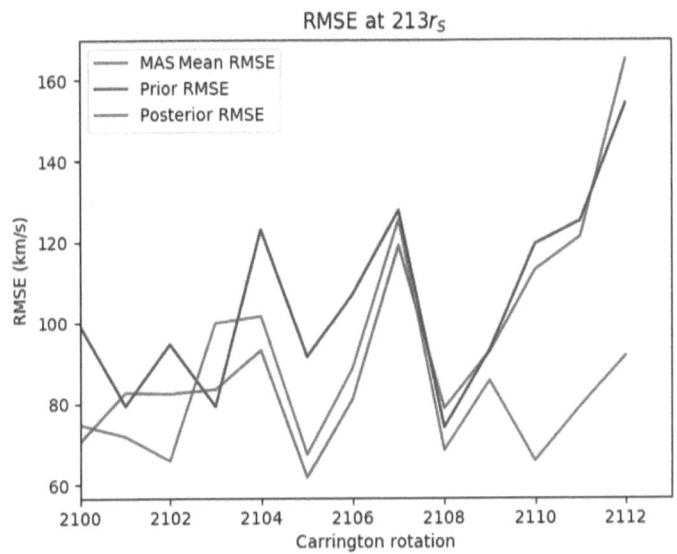

Figure 36 - The L1 version of RMSE

A model with a lower MAE is generally considered to be more accurate and to have a better fit for the data. However, it is important to note that MAE does not penalise large errors as heavily as RMSE, so it may not be as effective at identifying and correcting large errors in the model.

Cross-Validation

Cross-validation is a technique used to evaluate the performance of a machine-learning model. It involves dividing the dataset into a training set and a test set, training the model on the training set, and evaluating the model on the test set. This process is repeated multiple times, with different splits of the data, in order to get a better estimate of the model's performance.

There are several types of cross-validation techniques, including:

K-fold cross-validation: In k-fold cross-validation, the dataset is randomly partitioned into k folds, with k-1 folds used for training and the remaining fold used for testing. This process is repeated k times, with a different fold used for testing each time. The average performance across all k iterations is used to evaluate the model.

Stratified k-fold cross-validation: This is similar to k-fold cross-validation, but it ensures that the proportions of different classes in the folds represent the proportions in the entire dataset. This is particularly useful for imbalanced datasets where some classes are underrepresented.

Leave-one-out cross-validation: In leave-one-out cross-validation, the dataset is partitioned into n folds, with one observation in each fold and the remaining observations used for training. This process is repeated n times, with a different observation used for testing each time. The average performance across all n iterations is used to evaluate the model.

Cross-validation is a useful technique for evaluating the performance of a machine learning model because it helps to avoid overfitting and provides a more accurate estimate of the model's generalization error. It is an important step in the model development process and is commonly used in data science.

Predictive Power

Predictive power refers to a model's ability to accurately predict an event's outcome based on the data used to train the model. In data science, predictive power is an important evaluation metric for machine learning models because it determines the usefulness and practicality of the model for a particular task.

Several factors can affect the predictive power of a model, including the quality and quantity of the data used to train the model, the complexity of the model, and the choice of model parameters. A model with high predictive power can accurately predict the outcome of an event based on the data, while a model with low predictive power may be inaccurate or unreliable.

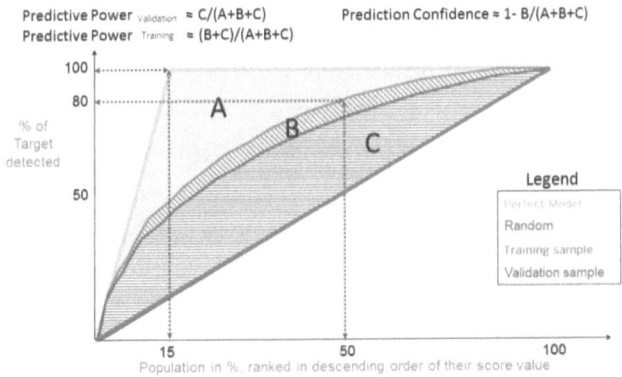

Figure 37 - Calculation of predictive power and prediction confidence

There are several ways to measure the predictive power of a model, including accuracy, precision, and recall. The specific measure used will depend on the goals and needs of the project.

In general, it is important to ensure that a model has high predictive power in order to make reliable and accurate predictions. This is achieved through careful model selection, training, and evaluation.

Understanding Data Analysis

Businesses and the government often employ data analysis to inform decisions. The data was produced when you sent the last email. You generated data when you went to the shopping site to make a purchase. Most likely, this information is kept someplace, generally on your computer or the business servers.

Have you ever considered the question, "What do individuals do with this data?" What a wonderful question. The study of data is a distinct field. It involves learning what a certain data collection is using. In order to identify a solution to a problem, data analysis requires processing, cleaning, and comprehending data.

Let's examine the next circumstance. The e-commerce site chooses which item to offer for sale during its next transaction. To boost sales, they are looking to market a well-liked product. A shopping website may use data analysis to identify the most popular goods so that they may choose which goods to offer for sale with better knowledge.

While humans judge based on their intuition, data analysis is predicated on the idea that figures can be trusted. The accuracy of someone's analysis rises with the amount of the dataset. Companies gather so much data because of this.

Who does data analysis?

As we saw in the section on data science roles, a data analyst answers the questions that businesses, governments, or other groups want to know. For example, it will be hard for the data analyst to figure out which product should be sold in an online store. Then, to solve the problem, they will use what they know about how professionals analyse data.

The tasks a data analyst does depend on what kind of business they work for. Governments use data analysis to do things like protect public health and predict changes in the economy. On the other hand, companies use data analysis for everything, from figuring out how you use an app to finding out which parts of a website user like best.

What do data analysts do?

Data analysts use tools like structured query language and mathematical libraries every single day. Most of the time, data analysts work with a specific set of data that has a set of values. A data engineer does this kind of work with data that needs to be analysed. Depending on the business's problem, it could be information about house sales, employee salaries, earthquakes, or something else.

First, data analysts look at the whole set of data. To find out what information it has and what conclusions can be made. They then use what they know about the data to analyse it differently, like using statistics in their research.

After the data analyst looks at the dataset, he will create a report with his findings. Their report should include a recommendation or a set of recommendations based on data that suggests an answer to a question.

Data analysis framework

A data analysis framework is a systematic approach that helps ensure that the data is analysed consistently and accurately. A data analysis framework typically includes the following steps:

Define the problem: Clearly define the problem or question that you are trying to answer with your data analysis.

Collect and prepare the data: Gather the data you will need for your analysis and ensure that it is clean and organised.

Explore and visualise the data: Explore the data to get a sense of its overall structure and patterns, and use visualisation techniques to help visualise and understand the data.

Model and analyse the data: Use statistical or machine learning techniques to analyse the data and draw conclusions.

Communicate the results: Clearly and effectively communicate the results of your analysis to others through reports, presentations, or other forms of communication.

Refine and iterate: Iterate your analysis as needed, incorporating new data or refining your approach to improve your results' accuracy.

Skills required for data analysis

Several skills are useful for analysing data:

Statistical analysis: Understanding statistical concepts such as mean, median, mode, standard deviation, and hypothesis testing can help you analyse and interpret data.

Encoding: To be a good data analyst, you must know how to write code. This is because analysing data is a very personal job. Each data set will be different. For a dataset to work well, you need to know how to clean, process, and analyse data in different ways. Most of the time, this is because a programming language like Python or R is being used.

Programming: As mentioned above, familiarity with programming languages such as Python, R, or SQL can be useful for manipulating and analysing data sets.

Data visualisation: The ability to create clear and effective charts, graphs, and other visualisations can help you communicate your findings effectively.

Attention to detail: Analysing data requires careful attention to detail, as small errors can have significant consequences.

Critical thinking: The ability to think critically and analyse data objectively is essential for producing accurate and unbiased results.

Communication: Effectively communicating your findings to others through written reports or presentations is important for sharing your insights and persuading others of your conclusions.

Storytelling with data

The American Bureau of Labor Statistics says[9] that between 2020 and 2030, the number of jobs for research analysts is expected to grow by 25%, much faster than the average for all jobs. Many companies have started putting "data storytelling" on their analyst job descriptions as a required skill. Others have hired data storytellers to add to the skills of their existing analytics teams. You can stand out as a well-rounded candidate if you know how to analyse data and explain what you've learned.

Benefits of storytelling with data

Today, we're surrounded by data and find it hard to make sense of it. Data-driven storytelling is a useful tool that shows the data and gives it context, meaning, relevance, and clarity to help the audience understand it and get value from it.

Here are some reasons why data storytelling is a good way to get your point across:

- Data stories add value by giving data meaning and context so that the audience can put the pieces together and turn numbers into useful insights. The insights, in turn, make it easier to make decisions and get things done.
- By using numbers and facts, you can back up your claims and make your content seem more reliable. This helps your audience trust you and makes it more likely that they'll agree with your point of view.
- Using your own and other people's data to make data stories helps you stand out and get people's attention.

In a world full of recycled content, unique ideas, useful perspectives, and unexpected angles help you cut through the noise.

- The graphic elements appeal to the media, making it more likely that high-profile publications or influential people will pick up your content. This will help you raise awareness of your brand, reach new audiences, and position your brand as a leader in its field.

- You use both sides of the brain when you combine narrative and visual elements. This simultaneously gives your audience a logical and emotional experience, which helps them understand, remember, and like the information.

- Different methods, such as interactive data visualisation, can help get people even more interested. For example, you could help them come to a conclusion or look at the part of the data story that interests them the most.

- Data-driven storytelling is versatile. It can be used in annual reports, brochures, case studies, presentations, videos, website content, white papers, social media posts, and more for both internal and external communication.

What is data storytelling?

Data storytelling is effectively sharing insights from a dataset through stories and pictures. It can help your audience understand data insights and move them to act.

There are three main parts to telling a story with data:

Data: Your data story is built on a thorough analysis of correct and complete data. When you use descriptive, diagnostic, predictive, and prescriptive analysis on data, you can get a full picture of what it means.

Narrative: A verbal or written narrative, also called a "story-line," is used to explain what you've learned from the data, what's happening around it, and what you want your audience to do.

Visualisations: Showing your data and story visually can help you tell its story in a way that is clear and easy to remember. These can be graphs, pictures, videos, or charts.

Data storytelling can be used internally or externally. For example, user data can be used to show that a product needs to be changed (for instance, to create a compelling case for buying your product to potential customers).

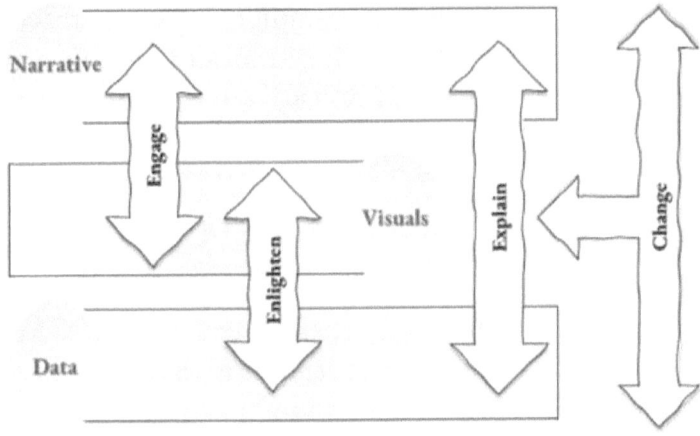

Figure 38 - Data storytelling framework

How the storytelling with data work?

Storytelling with data involves using data, visuals, and other forms of evidence to communicate a message or convey a narrative. Here are some tips for storytelling with data:

Start with a clear objective: Identify the key message or story you want to tell with your data, and make sure all of your data and visuals support that objective.

Choose the right data: Select relevant data that supports your message. Avoid using too much data or using data that is not directly related to your objective.

Use clear and effective visuals: Use charts, graphs, and other visuals to help illustrate your data and make it easier for others to understand. Choose appropriate visuals for the data and ensure they are accurate and well-labelled.

Use storytelling techniques: Use techniques such as establishing a problem, introducing a solution, and highlighting the benefits to structure your narrative and engage your audience.

Keep it simple: Avoid using jargon or overly technical language, and aim for clarity and simplicity in your presentation.

Practice and revise: Practice your storytelling with data in front of a test audience and revise your approach as needed to ensure that it is effective and engaging.

Data storytelling techniques

Storytelling is a powerful tool that great leaders use to get people to follow them, and great writers use it to create great works of literature. If you are just starting to write and tell stories, here are some tips that can help you make your stories stronger and keep your audience interested:

1. Choose a clear main point: A good story usually builds up to a moral or message at the end. When you're writing a story, you should clearly know where it's going. If your story has a strong moral message, you'll want to point people in the right direction. When telling a funny story, you might build up to a twist that will make everyone in the room laugh out loud. If you want to tell an interesting story, try building up the drama and suspense until the story's climax. No matter your story, you should be very clear on the main idea or plot point your story is built around.

2. Embrace conflict: If you want to tell a good story, you can't avoid conflict. Conflict is what makes plots interesting, and

if you want to be a better storyteller, you have to be open to conflict and drama. Great storytellers put their main characters in
situations where they deal with all kinds of problems. For people
to be happy with a happy ending, they must see the main characters work hard to get what they want. It's okay to be mean to your
main characters. It's necessary.

3. Have a clear structure: There are many different ways to
structure a story, but every story needs a beginning, middle, and
end. On a more detailed level, a good story will start with an "in-
citing incident," then build to a "climax," and end with a "satis-
fying resolution." Many books and online resources can help you
learn more about these terms and other ways to tell a story. You
can learn more about how stories are put together by reading and
watching stories by great storytellers and by laying out your own
stories on paper so you can see how they are put together.

4. Mine your personal experiences: Think about the important things that have happened to you in real life and how you
could turn them into stories. Whether you are telling a true story
based on your own life or not, you can always use your life to
come up with ideas for new stories.

5. Engage your audience: You have to connect with your
audience if you want to tell a good story, but how you do that
depends a lot on the type of story you're telling. If you're reading
a short story to a group of people, you might want to try taking
your eyes off the page every once in a while to look at the people
in the room. When you're recording a podcast that tells a story, a
lot depends on how expressive your voice is and how well you
can show emotion with your tone. No matter how you tell your
story, you should think about who will hear it.

6. Observe good storytellers: Your personal stories will always be unique and about you, but there's no better way to learn
how to write and tell a story than to watch great storytellers do it.
Most of us know people who can tell stories interestingly and
eloquently. Whether it's a family member who tells you stories
about their childhood at dinner or a local politician who is great

at public speaking, you've probably met more than a few good storytellers. Look for people who can tell good stories and learn from what you see. How do they make a story that works?

7. Limit your story's scope: When telling a true story from your own life, it can be hard to decide which parts are the most important. People often try to include every little detail and overwhelm their audience with facts that take away from the story's main point. Choose a clear beginning and end for your story, and then write the important plot points as bullet points between them. Trust that your audience will be able to follow your story, and don't give them too much background information or plot points that go off in a different direction.

Understanding business analytics

First, let's talk about how data analytics differs from traditional analytics. People often use the terms interchangeably, but there is a difference. Traditional data analytics is looking at and making predictions based on a huge amount of data. Business data analytics, sometimes called "business analytics," takes this idea and applies it to business insight. Business content and tools are often built to speed up the analysis process.

In particular, business analytics is the study of:

- Getting and processing business data from the past
- Using this data to find trends, patterns, and causes
- Using these ideas to make business decisions that are based on data

In other words, "data analytics" is more of an umbrella term for how analytics is done today. Business analytics has a narrower focus, and as the amount of data in the world has grown, it has become more common and more important for businesses worldwide.

Using cloud analytics tools, companies can combine data from different departments, such as sales, marketing, human resources, and finance, to get a single view showing how one department's numbers can affect the numbers from another department. Also, tools like visualisation, predictive insights, and scenario modelling give everyone in an organisation a wide range of unique insights.

Tools for business analytics

Business analytics tools handle the parts of crunching data and making insights through reports and visuals, but the process starts with the infrastructure for getting the data in. Many parts of business data analytics work together to give insights. Here is a typical flowchart for the business analytics process:

No matter where the data comes from—IoT devices, apps, spreadsheets, or social media—it needs to be gathered and put in one place so it can be used. Using a cloud database makes it much easier to gather information.

Data mining: Once data arrives and is stored (usually in a data lake), it needs to be sorted and processed. Machine learning algorithms can speed this up by recognising patterns and actions done repeatedly, such as setting up metadata for data from specific sources. This frees data scientists to focus on getting insights instead of doing manual tasks.

What is going on, and why is it going on? This is what descriptive analytics is all about. Answering these questions is what descriptive data analytics does to help people understand the story behind the data.

Predictive analytics: When business analytics tools have enough data and have processed enough descriptive analytics, they can start to build predictive models based on trends and historical context. So, these models can be used to help make business and organisational decisions in the future.

Visualisation and reporting: Tools for visualisation and reporting can help break down numbers and models so that they are easy to understand. This not only makes it easier to give presentations, but these kinds of tools can also help anyone, from experienced data scientists to business users, find new insights quickly.

Business intelligence vs business analytics

At first glance, it might not seem like there is much difference between business intelligence and business analytics. There is some overlap between the two, but there is still a big difference between business analytics and business intelligence that needs to be explained.

Business analytics uses next-generation technologies like machine learning, data visualisation, and artificial intelligence to make predictions based on data about how likely things are to happen in the future. Business intelligence uses historical and current data to figure out what happened in the past and now. On the other hand, business analytics builds on business intelligence and tries to predict what might happen in the future smartly.

What is cloud analytics?

Cloud analytics uses computing resources and services to analyse data and generate insights. Cloud analytics allows data to be stored, processed, and analysed in the cloud rather than on a local computer or server.

This allows organisations to scale their analytics capabilities as needed and take advantage of the flexibility and cost-effectiveness of the cloud.

Cloud analytics can be performed using a variety of tools and services, such as data warehouses, data lakes, business intelligence platforms, and machine learning platforms. These tools and services can be accessed over the internet, enabling users to analyse data from anywhere and on any device.

Cloud analytics has become increasingly popular in recent years due to its benefits, including the ability to quickly and easily access and analyse large amounts of data, the ability to scale analytics resources as needed, and the cost-effectiveness of using cloud resources.

What is data intelligence?

Data intelligence uses data, analytics, and related technologies to generate insights and inform decision-making. It involves the collection, organisation, analysis, and interpretation of data to gain a better understanding of a particular subject or problem.

Data intelligence can be applied in a wide range of industries and settings, including business, healthcare, government, and education. It can identify trends and patterns, discover new opportunities, optimise processes, and make more informed decisions.

Data intelligence relies on the use of advanced analytics techniques, such as machine learning and artificial intelligence, to analyse and interpret data. It also requires strong data management practices, including data governance, quality, and security.

Businesses and organisations collect data for intelligence from various sources, such as business performance metrics, data mining from customers and users, and other descriptive sources.

Data intelligence is different from business intelligence, which is more about putting data in order and presenting it in a way that makes it easy to understand and get business intelligence insights. Instead, data intelligence is more about how information is analysed.

What does it mean to integrate data?

Data integration is gathering information from different sources so users can see it all in one place. Data integration is to make data easier for systems and users to access, use, and process. When done right, data integration can lower IT costs, free up resources, improve data quality, and encourage innovation without making big changes to existing apps or data structures.

IT organisations have always had to integrate, but the potential benefits have never been as high as they are now.

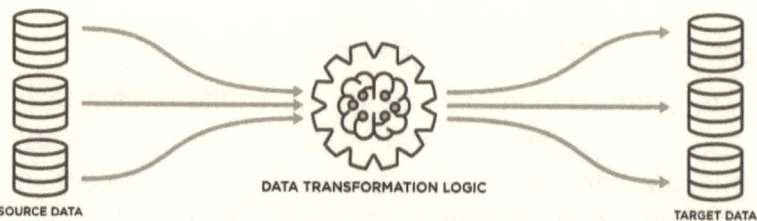

Figure 39 - Data integration

Companies that can integrate their data well have a lot of advantages over their competitors, such as:

- Reduced the need to change and combine data sets by hand, which increased operational efficiency.
- Better data quality with automated data transformations that apply business rules to data.
- More useful insights can be gained from data that can be looked at thoroughly.

A digital business is built around data and the algorithms that process it. It gets the most value out of its information assets, which can come from anywhere in the business ecosystem at anytime. In a digital business, data and related services move freely across the IT landscape while staying safe. Data integration gives you a full picture of all the information moving through an organisation and prepares your data for analysis.

Understanding data warehouse

A data warehouse is a central repository of data that is used for reporting and data analysis. It is designed to support the efficient querying and analysis of data and is typically used to support decision-making and strategic planning within an organisation.

Data warehouses are designed to handle large volumes of data and support complex queries and are typically optimised for fast performance and efficient data access. They often store data from multiple sources, such as transactional databases, log files, and external data sources, and can include data from both structured and unstructured sources.

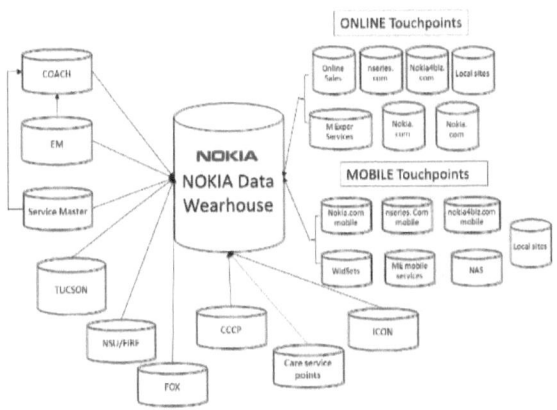

Figure 40 - Data warehouse example

Data warehouses typically use a multidimensional data model, which allows users to analyse data along multiple dimensions, such as time, location, and product. They also often use pre-aggregation, which involves pre-calculating and storing summary data to support faster querying and analysis.

To ensure that data in a data warehouse is accurate and up-to-date, it is typically updated regularly through ETL (extract, transform, load), which involves extracting data from various sources, cleaning and changing it, and loading it into the data warehouse.

ETL (Extract, Transform, Load)

ETL (extract, transform, load) is a process used to load data from various sources into a data warehouse or other centralised data repository. The ETL process consists of three main steps:

Extract: The first step in the ETL process is to extract data from various sources, such as transactional databases, log files, and external data sources. This typically involves using SQL queries or other methods to extract the data from the source systems.

Transform: Once the data has been extracted, it needs to be cleaned, transformed, and restructured to fit the structure and format of the target data repository. This may involve filtering out unnecessary data, merging data from multiple sources, and converting data types.

Load: The final step in the ETL process is to load the transformed data into the target data repository. This typically involves using SQL or other methods to insert the data into the appropriate tables in the data warehouse or other data repository.

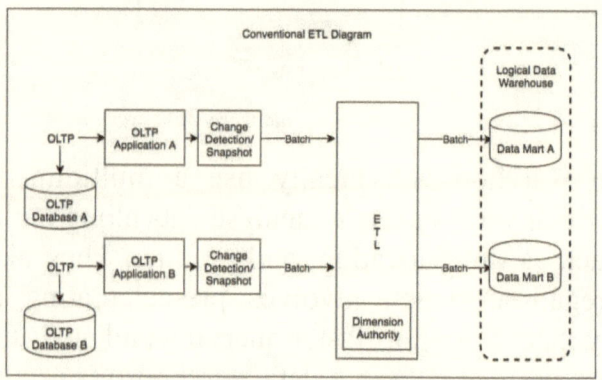

Figure 41 - ETL (Extract, Transform, Load)

The ETL process is an important part of data warehousing and is used to ensure that data in the data warehouse is accurate, up-to-date, and consistent with the source systems. ETL processes are typically automated and run regularly to ensure that the data warehouse data is always current.

140

Technologies can be used for data analysis

Yes, many technologies and tools can be used for data analysis, depending on the specific needs and characteristics of the data. Some common technologies and tools that may be used for data analysis include:

Spreadsheets: Spreadsheets, such as Microsoft Excel or Google Sheets, can be used for basic data analysis tasks, such as calculating summary statistics, creating pivot tables, and visualising data using charts and graphs.

Data visualisation tools: Data visualisation tools, such as Tableau or QlikView, are designed specifically for creating interactive and visually appealing charts, graphs, and dashboards from data. These tools can explore and analyse data, identify trends and patterns, and communicate insights.

Programming languages: Programming languages, such as Python or R, are often used for more advanced data analysis tasks, allowing you to write custom scripts and functions for manipulating and analyzing data. These languages also provide various libraries and packages for data manipulation, visualisation, and statistical analysis.

Machine learning frameworks: Machine learning frameworks, such as TensorFlow or PyTorch, can be used to build and train machine learning models on data and to make predictions or recommendations based on the data.

Business intelligence tools: Business intelligence (BI) tools, such as Power BI or SAP BusinessObjects, are designed to help organisations manage, analyse, and report on data from multiple sources. These tools may provide data visualisation, dashboard creation, and modelling features.

By using a combination of these technologies and tools, you can effectively analyse and make sense of your data.

Understanding Data Analytics

Data analytics uses data, statistical algorithms, and related technologies to uncover insights and inform decision-making. It involves collecting, organising, and analysing data to identify trends, patterns, and relationships, generate insights, and inform decision-making.

Data analytics can be applied in various industries and settings, including business, healthcare, government, and education. It can be used to optimise processes, identify new opportunities, and make more informed decisions.

There are several different types of data analytics, including descriptive analytics, diagnostic analytics, predictive analytics, and prescriptive analytics.

Descriptive analytics involves using data to describe and summarise past events, while diagnostic analytics involves using data to identify the root cause of a problem or issue.

Predictive analytics involves using data to predict future events, while prescriptive analytics involves using data to identify the best action to take in a given situation.

Data analytics relies on advanced techniques, such as machine learning and artificial intelligence, to analyse and interpret data. It also requires strong data management practices, including data governance, quality, and security.

Data analysis vs data analytics

Data analysis and data analytics are often used interchangeably, but they can refer to slightly different things.

Data analysis uses data, statistical algorithms, and related technologies to uncover insights and inform decision-making. It involves collecting, organising, and analysing data to identify trends, patterns, and relationships, generate insights, and inform decision-making.

Data analytics is a broader term that uses data, analytics, and related technologies to generate insights and inform decision-making. It encompasses various activities, including data collection, cleaning and preparation, visualisation, statistical analysis, and machine learning.

In general, data analysis is a specific type of data analytics that focuses on the analysis and interpretation of data, while data analytics is a broader term that includes data analysis as well as other activities related to working with data.

Data analytics framework

In order to effectively handle and optimise massive amounts of data, analytics frameworks must be implemented. They use modern data technology and streamlined procedures to provide plans for business operations that are rich in insights. Data was siloed, and efficiency barriers were not eliminated because of them in older models. In order to stay competitive, businesses need to understand and effectively utilise current data analytics frameworks.

Explaining the concept of a data analytics framework: Having a solid mechanism in place for handling data analytics efficiently and effectively is what a data analytics framework is all about. However, there are several meanings attached to the phrase.

Data analytics framework descriptions may sometimes include discussions of management procedures and best practices. Two prominent cases are the Cross-Industry Standard Process for Data Mining (CRISP-DM) recommendations and the Sample, Explore, Modify, Model, and Assess (SEMMA) method. Data analytics tools like Teradata Vantage and emerging data trends like the data mesh design pattern are also sometimes mentioned when this word is used.

A data analytics framework, in this context, is a combination of methods and tools for analysing data. Companies will have different policies and procedures, and their answers to problems will be unique. While data analytics frameworks may vary in specifics, they all have a common objective: to assist businesses in making the most of analytics. Analysing data without a proper framework in today's competitive corporate environment is unacceptable.

Applications of data analytics frameworks: In most cases, businesses have a particular goal in mind while developing their data analytics frameworks. Initially, this objective might be rather simple, such as "What business results do we aim to accomplish for the firm via data analytics?" After that, data teams specialise in a variety of tasks.

Evaluation of results: In fact, this is one of the most prevalent applications of analytics and the frameworks that enable them. Companies need to keep their finger on the financial pulse, and one way to do so is by collecting and analysing key performance indicators (KPIs).

With the use of a data analytics framework, data teams may track metrics like the number of daily active users, level of engagement, and rate of new user adoption for a customer-facing app, in addition to more broad performance indicators like profitability across business divisions.

Manufacturing process improvement: Creating anything fresh in isolation is no longer feasible. Sales records, key performance indicators (KPIs) for rivals' success or failure with a comparable product, demand analyses, projected product failures, and many other data types are necessary for development.

Developers now have access to much more information because of the capacity of numerous contemporary technologies (from smartphones and medical wearables to current automobiles) to capture data on user behaviour. With the help of data analytics frameworks, product teams may use this heterogeneous data to their advantage, gleaning insights that can be used to correct course and improve future product design.

Using past data, mechanics can anticipate repairs: Manufacturers and other heavy industrial firms may evaluate machine health, anticipate the possibility of failure, and plan priority repairs with the help of predictive maintenance systems. Data analytics frameworks provide analysts with the structure they need to collect all the data required to generate these predictions, including the age of the equipment, the number of repairs it has undergone, signs of wear and tear, the efficacy of maintenance procedures, and so on. This reduces the likelihood of unscheduled downtime and keeps production on pace.

Advantages of a highly advanced analytics framework that is cloud-ready: There is great potential for your business to reap many rewards from implementing a data analytics framework founded on solid data science concepts and backed by agile, dependable technology. The most prominent ones are as follows:

Data can be integrated and used more quickly: Multiple data types may coexist in a cloud-centric analytics framework, and various analysis techniques can be implemented.

These enhancements make it possible to speed up data integration and efficient utilisation, reducing analysis time and eliminating or greatly reducing performance bottlenecks. As a result, more time is available for developing novel uses for data because processing, preparing, and reconfiguring them takes less effort.

Quick implementation and use also make real-time data processing possible. Customer service may be enhanced, as can internal cooperation, creativity, and productivity.

Less data transmission and duplication: If your company adopts a state-of-the-art, cloud-based data analytics framework, it can store, retrieve, and use all of its data without worrying about formatting, duplicating, or relocating any of it. You may skip the hassle of collecting and converting data into a usable format and instead focus on analysis, application, and new ideas. Ultimately, this will allow for a holistic perspective on the company and the development of a reliable, trusted source of information (SSOT).

Unbounded scalability: A data analytics platform that can be scaled up or down on short notice is crucial in today's fast-paced, ever-changing business world to keep up with your company's and your customers' ever-evolving requirements. To a T, it is what a cloud-based framework provides. Cloud analytics solutions enable you to pay for what you need, while the tools used in more conventional analytics frameworks might be costly or entail fixed pricing schemes. Savings in expenses may also be a result of this scalability.

The Future in Sight: The market for business analytics already has a wide variety of methods and a plethora of supplementary tools, and it is only expected to expand. Some important trends to keep an eye on are:

As more corporate users become interested in using analytics without the assistance of a data scientist, analyst, or engineer, the demand for self-service reporting grows.

Eventually, more businesses will have the computing power to implement deep learning, the most sophisticated ML based on multi-layer neural networks. As demand for real-time streaming analytics grows, experts predict that the data fabric idea will gain traction.

Given the exponential growth of both the volume and variety of data being generated, it is becoming evident that successful data analytics frameworks will need to use cloud computing capabilities. Data teams should keep an eye on these and other changes to see whether they need to rethink their data analytics frameworks and architecture. But there's one development that's too enormous to ignore.

Different types of data analytics

There are several different types of data analytics, including:
- Descriptive analytics

- Diagnostic analytics
- Predictive analytics
- Prescriptive analytics
- Cognitive analytics

Let's look into each of them in more detail:

What is descriptive analytics?

Descriptive analytics is a type of data analytics that involves the use of data to describe and summarise past events. It uses charts, graphs, and tables to visualise and understand data. It can be used to identify trends and patterns in the data and to summarise data in a way that is easy to understand and can help inform decision-making.

Examples of descriptive analytics include:

- Calculating and displaying summary statistics, such as the mean, median, or standard deviation of a data set
- Creating charts and graphs to visualise data and identify trends and patterns
- Generating reports and dashboards to display key metrics and highlight trends or patterns in the data

Descriptive analytics is a foundational element of data analytics and is often the first step in the data analytics process. It is typically followed by more advanced analytics, such as diagnostic, predictive, or prescriptive analytics, which build on the insights and trends identified through descriptive analytics.

Understanding diagnostic analysis

Diagnostic analytics is a type of data analytics that involves using data to identify the root cause of a problem or issue. It involves using techniques such as root cause analysis and fault tree analysis to understand the underlying causes of a pain, and can be used to identify potential solutions. This can be particularly useful for identifying problems that are difficult to diagnose or that have multiple contributing factors.

Examples of diagnostic analytics include:

- Using data to identify the root cause of a production issue in a manufacturing plant
- Analysing customer feedback data to identify the root cause of customer dissatisfaction
- Using data to identify the root cause of a decline in sales or revenue

Diagnostic analytics often builds on the insights and trends identified through descriptive analytics and can be used to identify potential solutions or areas for improvement. It is a valuable tool for identifying and addressing organisational problems and issues.

Predictive analytics

Predictive analytics is a type of data analytics that involves using data and statistical algorithms to make predictions about future events. It involves analyzing past data to identify patterns and trends that can be used to forecast future outcomes or trends.

Predictive analytics can be used to make informed decisions about resource allocation, risk management, and other strategic planning activities. It is often used in a variety of industries, including finance, healthcare, and marketing.

Examples of predictive analytics include:

- Using data to forecast future sales or revenue for a company
- Analysing data to identify patterns and trends that can be used to predict future customer behaviour
- Using machine learning algorithms to predict the likelihood of a particular outcome or event occurring

Predictive analytics relies on advanced techniques like machine learning and artificial intelligence to analyse and interpret data. It is an increasingly important tool for organisations looking to make informed, data-driven decisions. It requires large amounts of data and strong statistical skills to be effective.

Prescriptive analytics

Prescriptive analytics is a type of data analytics that involves using data to identify the best course of action to take in a given situation. It combines predictive analytics with optimisation algorithms to identify the optimal action based on available data.

Prescriptive analytics can be used to help organisations make more informed, data-driven decisions. It is often used to identify the best course of action to take in complex or uncertain situations and can help organisations make better use of their resources and optimise their operations.

Examples of prescriptive analytics include:

- Using data to identify the most cost-effective transportation route for a delivery
- Analysing data to identify the optimal inventory levels for a manufacturing plant
- Using data to identify the most effective marketing strategies for a business

Prescriptive analytics relies on advanced techniques like machine learning and artificial intelligence to analyse and interpret data. It requires large amounts of data and strong analytical skills to be effective.

It is an increasingly important tool for organisations looking to optimise their operations and make informed data-driven decisions.

Cognitive analytics

Cognitive analytics is a type of data analytics that involves the use of artificial intelligence and machine learning techniques to analyse and interpret data. It involves the development of algorithms that can learn from data and make decisions or recommendations based on their learning.

Cognitive analytics is often used to automate decision-making and identify patterns and data trends that may not immediately appear to humans. It can be used to analyse large volumes of data and identify patterns and relationships that cannot be identified through manual analysis.

Examples of cognitive analytics include:

- Using machine learning algorithms to analyse customer feedback data and identify patterns or trends
- Analyzing data from sensors to identify patterns or trends that may indicate a problem or issue
- Using artificial intelligence to automate decision-making and recommend actions based on data analysis

Cognitive analytics requires strong data management practices and advanced analytics skills, including machine learning and artificial intelligence. It is an increasingly important tool for organisations looking to automate decision-making and make more informed data-driven decisions.

Tools that can be used for data analytics

Many technologies and tools can be used for data analytics, depending on the data's specific needs and characteristics and the analysis's goals. Some common technologies and tools that may be used for data analytics include:

Spreadsheets: Spreadsheets, such as Microsoft Excel or Google Sheets, can be used for basic data analytics tasks, such as calculating summary statistics, creating pivot tables, and visualising data using charts and graphs.

Data visualisation tools: Data visualisation tools, such as Tableau or QlikView, are explicitly designed for creating interactive and visually appealing charts, graphs, and dashboards from data. These tools can be used to explore and analyse data, identify trends and patterns, and communicate insights.

Programming languages: Programming languages, such as Python or R, are often used for more advanced data analytics tasks, as they allow you to write custom scripts and functions for manipulating and analysing data. These languages also provide a wide range of libraries and packages for data manipulation, visualisation, and statistical analysis.

Machine learning frameworks: Machine learning frameworks, such as TensorFlow or PyTorch, can be used to build and train machine learning models on data and to make predictions or recommendations based on the data.

Business intelligence tools: Business intelligence (BI) tools, such as Power BI or SAP BusinessObjects, are designed to help organisations manage, analyse, and report on data from multiple sources. These tools may provide data visualisation, dashboard creation, and modelling features.

Using these technologies and tools, you can effectively analyse and make sense of your data.

Data Cleaning

Data cleaning is identifying and correcting errors, inconsistencies, and missing values in data. It is an important step in the data analytics process, as dirty or incorrect data can lead to inaccurate or misleading insights and conclusions.

Data cleaning typically involves the following steps:

- ***Identifying errors and inconsistencies:*** This involves identifying and reviewing the data to identify errors, inconsistencies, and missing values. This may involve using tools such as data visualisation or statistical analysis to identify issues in the data.

- **Cleaning the data:** Once errors and inconsistencies have been identified, the data needs to be cleaned to correct these issues. This may involve tasks such as filling in missing values, correcting errors, or standardising data formats.

- ***Verifying the data:*** After the data has been cleaned, it is important to verify that the data is accurate and complete. This may involve reviewing the data again to ensure that all errors and inconsistencies have been corrected or using statistical techniques to validate the data.

- ***Documenting the cleaning process:*** It is important to document the data cleaning process, including any errors or inconsistencies that were identified and how they were corrected. This can help to ensure that the data cleaning process is transparent and reproducible.

Data cleaning is an ongoing process that should be performed regularly to ensure that the data is accurate and complete. It is an important step in the data analytics process, as it helps to ensure that the insights and conclusions generated from the data are accurate and reliable.

By "cleaning up" data, we mean making sure that every value in a dataset is valid and in the format the programmer specifies. To clean up "dirty data" is what "data cleansing" refers to.

Rarely does raw data arrive in a tidy, pre-packaged file that considers everything you'll need to do with the information. This is where "cleaning" comes in.

After receiving a dataset, the first thing a data scientist should do is clean it. They should make an effort to read through the dataset. To ensure its usability within the framework of their application.

An expert in data might learn a lot about the dataset while they are cleaning it. While cleaning up the dataset, the data scientist gains insight into the nature of the data, its structure, and the aspects of the dataset that they find objectionable.

Why is data cleaning so crucial?

Data scientists can get more reliable results from their analyses if they first take the time to clean up their data. Information discovery is the focus of a data specialist's work. Any conclusion a data scientist reaches using faulty input is certain to be off.

Also, cleaning up the data will save you time in the long run. Before analysing the data, it must first be cleaned. What this implies is that the data scientist analyses the data far in advance of reaching any conclusions. The data set will be put up in the way they specify.

The data scientist may proceed with the analysis when the data set is complete and error-free. That he won't have to go back and adjust improper formatting or delete wrong information. In the end, the goal of every data scientist is to have a complete and coherent dataset. Critical for reaching a sound judgement on the matter.

How do you get it all nice and tidy?

Data scientists all have their own unique methods for vetting and scrubbing raw data. The norms of various organisations vary. Before using the dataset in any analysis, ensure it has been properly cleaned.

Examine the void in the data.

Before beginning any analysis, data scientists want to have all the necessary data at their disposal. That's why, during the cleansing phase, the data analyst double-checks for any gaps. The data analyst may adjust their strategy accordingly if the information is unavailable. This demands careful consideration since it affects a data scientist's conclusions.

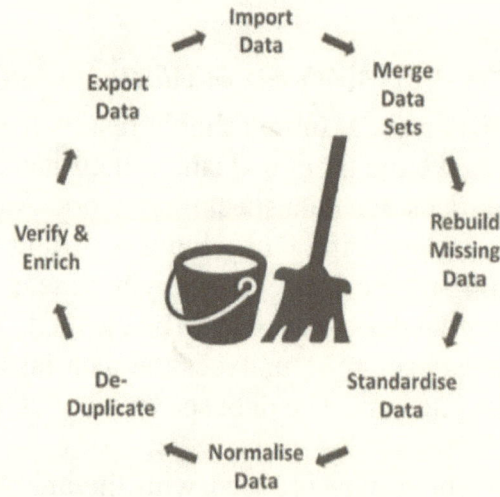

Figure 42 = Effective data cleaning

A data scientist may extrapolate from known numbers to fill in the gaps. A data scientist may use software to determine an average, for instance, if he wants such a figure. In other words, they shouldn't remove any analysis that relies on an average. The data scientist may ensure the algorithm can readily handle the dataset by including values like 0 in it. These values will fill in the blanks in the dataset, which may have been introduced due to sampling mistakes.

Clean up the data

Some of the information in the dataset is unnecessary. While extra information might be valuable in certain situations, it could also be a distraction for the data professional doing the study. The data scientist will remove any irrelevant information before beginning the study using data analysis tools. That will make their dataset more manageable by cutting down on its overall size.

Discard duplicates

Repeated information is likely to be included in the dataset as it is compiled. This may occur if the dataset was not checked at the time of collection or if data from other datasets were mixed.

The validity of the results may be guaranteed by eliminating superfluous information. If the dataset contains repeated information, some of the records may show a preference for a certain result. Consequently, the reliability of the final results will suffer as a result of this.

Data processing for emissions

The dataset may include estimates of emissions. The data analyst will check for emissions in the dataset. Perhaps there's a single blank value or a scratched record. There are two potential courses of action if the value is being ejected. An analyst may clean a data set of all emissions by simply removing the column containing such values. This is likely to be the case if there is little confidence in the ejection value. Furthermore, the data scientist may choose to verify the value. The data scientist may use this to double-check for input or collection problems before erasing a value.

There is no way to do data analysis without first cleaning the data. Cleaning occurs between data collection and analysis. The data scientist will do the cleansing procedure to guarantee that the dataset is complete, correct, and legitimate.

Data scientists would have to take time away from the dataset analysis to remedy simple data problems if the data weren't cleaned up beforehand. The examination of the data may get so muddled as a result that its original validity is compromised.

Documenting the cleaning process

Documenting the data cleaning process is an important step in any data analysis project, as it helps to ensure the integrity and quality of the data. Here are some steps you can follow to document your data-cleaning process:

- Create a document or spreadsheet to keep track of your data-cleaning process. This will allow you to reference your work and communicate it to others easily.
- Identify any errors or inconsistencies in the data. This may include missing values, incorrect data types, or outliers.
- Describe the steps you took to correct these errors or inconsistencies. This should include any functions or techniques you used to fix the data and any manual changes you made.
- Document any decisions you made during the data cleaning process. For example, explain your reasoning for selecting one over the others if you had to choose between multiple options for handling missing values.
- Keep track of any changes you make to the data. This will allow you to easily refer back to your work and understand the impact of your changes on the data.

- Save your cleaned data in a separate file or format, and keep a copy of the original data for reference.

Following these steps, you can create a comprehensive record of your data cleaning process, which will help you understand and communicate your work to others.

Best techniques for data cleaning

Several techniques can be used for data cleaning, depending on the specific needs and characteristics of the data. Here are some common techniques that may be used:

Handling missing values: This may involve replacing missing values with a placeholder value (e.g., 0 or "NA"), dropping rows or columns with missing values, or imputing missing values using statistical techniques such as mean imputation or linear regression.

Handling outliers: Outliers can significantly impact statistical analyses, and they may be caused by errors or by simple but unusual observations. Outliers can be detected using techniques such as box plots or z-scores, and they can be handled by dropping them, transforming them, or imputing values for them.

Fixing errors: Data may contain errors made during data entry, transmission, or other processes. These errors can be identified and corrected using techniques such as cross-checking against other sources, using regex to fix common formatting errors, or applying business logic to validate data values.

Normalising data: Normalisation refers to scaling and shifting data values to have a common scale and distribution. Normalization can be useful when comparing data from different sources or when using machine learning algorithms that assume a certain level of variance in the data.

Cleaning up formatting: Data may have inconsistent formatting, such as different date formats or inconsistent use of capitalisation. These issues can be addressed using string manipulation, regular expressions, and formatting functions.

Removing duplicates: Duplicate data can cause problems when analysing and visualising data, and it may be necessary to identify and remove duplicate rows or records. This can be done using techniques such as deduplication algorithms or by manually reviewing the data.

By combining these techniques, you can effectively clean and prepare your data for analysis.

Technologies can be used for data cleaning

Many technologies and tools can be used for data cleaning, depending on the specific needs and characteristics of the data. Here are some common technologies and tools that may be used:

Spreadsheets: Spreadsheets, such as Microsoft Excel or Google Sheets, are often used for basic data cleaning tasks, such as sorting and filtering data, removing duplicates, and fixing formatting issues.

Data wrangling tools: These tools, such as OpenRefine or Trifacta, are designed specifically for data cleaning and transformation tasks. These tools typically provide a user-friendly interface and a range of features for handling missing values, outliers, errors, and other common data issues.

Data visualisation tools: Data visualisation tools, such as Tableau or QlikView, can be useful for identifying and visualising patterns in data, which can help to identify errors or inconsistencies. These tools may also have features for cleaning and transforming data.

Programming languages: Programming languages, such as Python or R, can be used for more advanced data cleaning tasks, as they allow you to write custom scripts and functions for handling specific data issues. These languages also provide a wide range of libraries and packages for data manipulation, visualisation, and analysis.

Databases: Relational databases, such as MySQL or PostgreSQL, can be used to store and manage data, and they may provide features for data cleaning, such as the ability to update or delete data or to run queries to identify and fix errors.

By using a combination of these technologies and tools, you can effectively clean and prepare your data for analysis.

Data Mining

Data mining is discovering patterns and relationships in large datasets using specialised algorithms and statistical techniques. It is a crucial aspect of data analytics and is often used to extract valuable insights and knowledge from data.

Data mining is a term coined to transform raw data into useful and more understandable information. Many companies use data mining to find and analyse patterns in their marketing, revenue, expense, and sales data. This information is then used to make important marketing strategies and financial management decisions.[10]

The data mining process begins with companies collecting data and uploading it to the data warehouses where it is stored and managed. This information is transferred to software designed to sort the data and then sorted and displayed as a diagram, graph, or table. Often it also loads into the cloud for storage. Business analysts then study the data and decide how to organise and display it.

Data analysts do quite a lot of work to find these useful ideas. Typically, they are instructed to search for suitable data sets and variables to study, collect both structured and unstructured data, analyse and interpret data, and explain their findings to stakeholders in an understandable way.

Data mining involves the following steps:

Preprocessing: This involves cleaning and preparing the data for analysis, including handling missing values, identifying and fixing errors, and normalizing data.

Exploration: This involves exploring the data to understand its characteristics and identify patterns and relationships. This may involve visualising the data or using statistical techniques to identify trends and anomalies.

Modelling: This involves building statistical or machine-learning models to identify patterns and relationships in the data.

These models may make predictions or recommendations based on the data.

Evaluation: This involves evaluating the effectiveness and accuracy of the models and identifying any areas for improvement.

Deployment: This involves implementing the models in a production environment and using them to make decisions or take action based on the insights and knowledge extracted from the data.

Data mining can be applied to various applications, including marketing, finance, healthcare, and many others. It can identify trends and patterns in data, predict future outcomes, and make recommendations based on data-driven insights.

Data science vs data mining

Data mining and data science are related fields that involve working with data to extract insights and knowledge, but they are not the same thing.

Data mining is focused on discovering patterns and relationships in large datasets using specialised algorithms and statistical techniques. It is often used to identify trends and anomalies in data and to make predictions or recommendations based on the data.

Data science is a broader field that involves using a variety of techniques and tools to extract insights and knowledge from data. It includes data mining and other aspects such as data visualisation, machine learning, and statistical analysis.

Data science involves discovering patterns and relationships in data, understanding and interpreting the meaning and context of the data, and communicating the analysis results to stakeholders.

In summary, data mining is a specific technique within the field of data science, while data science is a more comprehensive field that encompasses a wider range of techniques and approaches for working with data.

Data mining process models

Data mining is a technique for gaining insights from unstructured data in a novel way. Data mining is used for various purposes, most commonly for corporate intelligence research, political model predictions, online ranking forecasts, weather pattern predicting, etc.

Business specialists use company operation intelligence studies to sift through massive amounts of data about a business operation or market to find previously unknown patterns and linkages. Businesses that rely on massive amounts of data often use data mining techniques to sift through all that information and find what they need.

When people talk about "data mining," they're typically referring to the standard manner in which data is presented and the different methods by which it may be used to answer specific questions or solve particular issues. Experts agree that the data mining regression model is the most widely used field. An expert miner initially analyses the data sets and formulates a definition for them. Experts widely use this model throughout the financial sector to forecast future market prices and trends.

The association rule is the basis of another influential data mining methodology. Data mining experts examine the datasets to see what features tend to occur together. It is assumed that a relationship exists between the two parts when they are found paired simultaneously. An electronics store, for instance, could notice that customers often buy a marker and pen along with a book. The data mining methodology provides rich details that might help a store manager boost sales by grouping similar items together.

Types of data mining models

- Predictive data mining models
- Descriptive data mining models

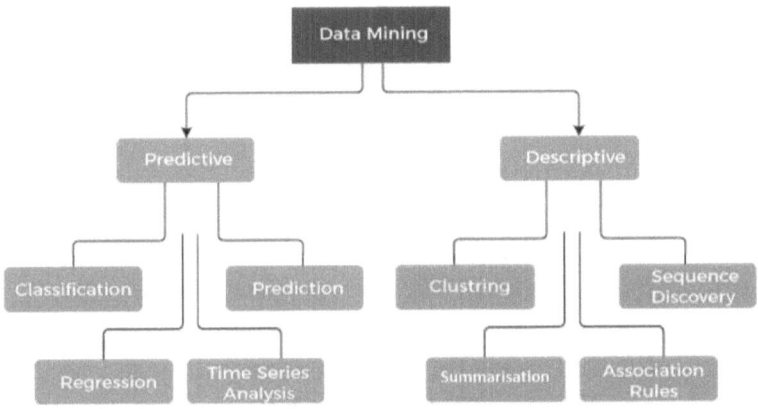

Figure 43 - Data mining models

Predictive data mining models

Using the findings from the many data sets that are already known, a predictive data mining model may make educated guesses as to the values of the data. Predictive modelling is so ubiquitous that it defies categorization as a distinct field of study. Predictive data mining methods rely heavily (but not only) on statistical modelling to make predictions.

High-risk individuals with conditions including congestive heart failure, high blood pressure, diabetes, infection, cancer, and so on are often identified using predictive modelling in the healthcare industry. In the auto insurance industry, it's used to determine who should pay for damages in the event of an accident.

Classification

In data mining, classification predicts the class or category of an instance or record based on its attributes or features. For example, a classification model might predict whether a customer is likely to churn based on their age, income, and previous purchasing history or whether a patient is likely to have a certain disease based on their symptoms, medical history, and test results.

Classification models are trained on a labelled data set with known class labels. The model learns to identify patterns and relationships between the attributes and the class labels, and it uses this knowledge to make predictions on new, unseen data.

Several classification algorithms include decision trees, random forests, support vector machines, and logistic regression. The choice of algorithm depends on the data's characteristics and the application's specific requirements.

Classification is a common task in data mining, and it is used in a wide range of applications, such as email filtering, fraud detection, customer segmentation, and medical diagnosis.

Prediction

In data mining, prediction uses data and statistical models to predict future outcomes or values based on past and present data. Prediction models are trained on historical data and learn to identify patterns and relationships that can be used to make predictions on new, unseen data.

Various techniques and algorithms can be used for prediction in data mining, including linear regression, logistic regression, decision trees, and machine learning algorithms such as support vector machines and neural networks. The choice of algorithm depends on the data's characteristics and the application's specific requirements.

Prediction is a common task in data mining, and it is used in a wide range of applications, such as financial forecasting, demand forecasting, and predictive maintenance.

Regression

In data mining, regression is a statistical technique used to predict a continuous numerical value, such as a price, revenue, or quantity. Regression models are trained on a labelled dataset, which consists of records with known output values (also known as the dependent variable). The model learns to identify patterns and relationships between the input variables (the independent variables) and the output values. It uses this knowledge to make predictions on new, unseen data.

There are several types of regression algorithms, including linear regression, logistic regression, and nonlinear regression. The choice of algorithm depends on the data's characteristics and the application's specific requirements.

Regression is a common task in data mining, and it is used in a wide range of applications, such as predicting the price of a house based on its characteristics, forecasting sales based on historical data, and estimating the risk of default for a loan applicant based on their credit history.

Time series analysis

Time series analysis is a statistical technique for analyzing and modelling data collected over time. Time series data consists of observations collected at regular intervals, such as daily sales data, monthly stock prices, or hourly temperature readings.

Time series analysis involves the following steps:

Descriptive analysis: This involves exploring and summarising the characteristics of the time series data, such as its trend, seasonality, and level of noise or random variation.

Modelling: This involves building statistical or machine learning models to represent the time series data and to identify patterns and relationships within the data.

Forecasting: This involves using the models to predict future values of the time series data.

There are several types of time series models, including autoregressive (AR) models, moving average (MA) models, and autoregressive moving average (ARMA) models. The choice of model depends on the data's characteristics and the application's specific requirements.

Time series analysis is a common task in data mining, and it is used in a wide range of applications, such as financial forecasting, demand forecasting, and predicting traffic patterns.

Descriptive data mining models

Using a descriptive model, one may identify and describe important data correlations and trends. Unlike a predictive model, a descriptive model does not try to extrapolate results to a larger sample or a random event.

In order to extrapolate to a larger population or random process, predictive models often make broad assumptions. Predictive models should provide prediction intervals and be cross-validated or demonstrate their efficacy in making predictions using data that was not integral to the model's development.

Clustering

Clustering is a type of unsupervised learning in which data is organised into groups (called clusters) based on similarities among the data points within a cluster. The goal of clustering is to split the data into groups such that data points within a group are more similar to each other than they are to data points in other groups.

Many different clustering algorithms exist, including k-means, hierarchical, and density-based clustering. Each of these algorithms works in another way, but they all aim to identify patterns in the data and group similar data points together.

One common use of clustering in data science is to segment a large dataset into smaller, more manageable groups for further analysis. For example, a marketing team might use clustering to segment their customer base into different groups based on their purchasing habits so that they can tailor their marketing campaigns to each group. Clustering can also identify underlying patterns in data that may not be immediately obvious, such as grouping together medical patients with similar symptoms or documents that cover similar topics.

Clustering is a useful tool for exploring and understanding data, providing valuable insights that can help inform decision-making.

Sequence discovery

Sequence discovery, also known as sequential pattern mining, is the process of identifying patterns in data that represent sequences of events or actions. These patterns can provide valuable insights into how the data is organised and how it may be related to other data.

In data science, sequence discovery is often used to analyse sequential data, such as time series data or transactional data. For example, a retailer might use sequence discovery to identify patterns in customer purchase data, such as which products are typically purchased together or in what order they are typically purchased. This can help the retailer understand consumer behaviour and make more informed decisions about inventory management and marketing campaigns.

Several algorithms and techniques are used for sequence discovery, including association rule mining, Markov models, and hidden Markov models. These algorithms typically involve identifying frequent patterns in the data and using these patterns to make predictions about future events or actions.

Overall, sequence discovery is a useful tool for data scientists working with sequential data, as it can help identify trends and patterns that may not be immediately obvious and provide valuable insights into data relationships and behaviour.

Summarisation

Summarisation is reducing a large dataset or document to a more minor, more digestible form while retaining the most important information. In data mining, summarisation is often used to reduce the complexity of a dataset, make it more manageable, and extract key insights or trends.

There are several techniques used for summarisation in data mining, including:

Aggregation: This involves grouping together similar data points and calculating summary statistics, such as mean, median, or mode.

Sampling: This involves selecting a representative subset of the data and analysing it to conclude the larger dataset.

Data reduction: This involves applying algorithms or techniques to identify and remove redundant or irrelevant data while preserving the most important information.

Text summarisation: This involves reducing the size of a document or text by extracting the most important sentences or phrases.

Summarisation can effectively understand a large and complex dataset and help data scientists focus on the most important information and trends. It is often used as a preprocessing step before more advanced analysis, or modelling techniques are applied.

Association rules

Association rules are a data mining technique used to identify patterns and relationships within large datasets. These rules describe the statistical relationships between different items or variables in a dataset and can be used to predict future events or behaviours.

An association rule is typically written as "if X occurs, then Y is likely to occur," where X and Y are items or variables in the dataset. For example, a retailer might use association rules to identify patterns in customer purchase data, such as "if a customer buys bread, they are likely also to buy butter."

Association rules are often used to identify market trends and make informed decisions about inventory management and marketing campaigns. They can also be used to identify fraud or anomalies within a dataset.

Several algorithms and techniques are used to generate association rules, including the Apriori and FP-growth algorithms. These algorithms work by identifying frequent patterns in the data and using these patterns to generate rules that can be used to make predictions.

Association rules are a powerful tool for data mining, as they can help identify important patterns and relationships within large datasets and provide valuable insights for decision-making.

Data Modelling

In the data science lifecycle, we briefly touched on this topic. In this section, we will attempt a deep dive.

Data modelling is the use of language and symbols to represent data and the flow of that data in order to create a simplified representation of a software system and the data pieces it includes. An organisation may better satisfy its information demands using data modelling. If you need to create a new database or refactor an old one, you may use a data model as a guide.

Think of a data model as a flowchart, where each node represents a data entity, and each line represents an attribute or connection between entities. Before writing any code, it aids data management and analytics groups in laying out the specifics of what information is needed from apps and spotting any mistakes in the development strategy.

Data models may also be developed by reverse engineering, which involves obtaining the necessary information from working systems. This is done to build schemas for raw data sets stored in data lakes or NoSQL databases and to record the structure of relational databases that were constructed ad hoc without prior data modelling to enable particular analytics applications.

The use of data modelling

An integral part of any data management strategy, data modelling is a crucial skill. The document details the attributes of the data items that will be incorporated into applications and the database or file system structures used to process, store, and manage the data. A visual depiction of data sets and their business context is provided, which aids in identifying information requirements for various business activities.

Data models, data flow diagrams, architectural blueprints, a consistent data language, and other artefacts are essential parts of data architecture. Data modelling may also be used with governance initiatives to provide consistent internal data definitions and standards. Furthermore, it is crucial in data architecture procedures, including cataloguing data assets, tracing their journey across IT networks, and developing a theoretical framework for managing data.

Data modellers, architects, and other data management specialists have historically collaborated with business analysts, executives, and end users to develop comprehensive data models. However, data modelling is now also essential for data scientists and analysts working on BI apps or more sophisticated data science and analytics tools.

Data model types

Models are usually developed in stages as organisations design new databases and applications. Business ideas and procedures, relevant data items and their properties and connections, and technological frameworks for handling the data are each represented in their own models by data modellers. In general, there are four categories of data models, each of which includes the following elements:

Conceptual data model

Informational model in theory. This is an overarching diagram of the business or analytics procedures that a system will facilitate. It lays out the types of data required, the relationships between various business organisations, and the rules governing these relationships. Business leaders mostly use conceptual data models to foresee the functionality of a system and verify that it satisfies those requirements. Conceptual models may be used with any data store or software platform.

Logical data model

This is the intuitive representation of data. A more concrete logical model may be developed with a completed conceptual data model. Technically speaking, logical data models represent the data and demonstrate the relationships between data elements. They outline the specifics of data structures, such as their properties, keys, data types, and other defining features. Logical models are used by the technical side of an organisation to comprehend necessary applications and database architectures better. In contrast to conceptual models, however, they are not tied to any specific technological environment.

Physical data model

Database designers use physical data models to design databases and generate the database schema. The development of a physical data model starts with a logical model. The physical models are tailored to the DBMS or application software being used. They specify how information is to be organised for storage in a database or a file system. Database Management System components include tables, columns, fields, indexes, constraints, and triggers.

Methodologies for modelling data

Data modelling first appeared in the 1960s, when databases were being utilised increasingly on mainframes and, later, minicomputers. It let businesses implement data processing and management practises that were consistent, repeatable, and developed systematically. Even if this remains true, as databases and computers have progressed, so too have the methods used to generate them.

Common data modelling strategies across time include those that newer methods have mostly superseded.

Modelling data in a hierarchical structure

Data in hierarchical models is structured like a tree, with parent and child nodes. This is a one-to-many modelling technique since each child record may have only one parent. The hierarchical structure first appeared in mainframe databases, the most well-known being IBM's Information Management System (IMS). Although relational data models began to replace hierarchical ones in the 1980s, many companies continue to utilise IMS. XML, short for Extensible Markup Language, also uses a hierarchical structure today.

Modelling networks using data

This was another well-liked data modelling approach in mainframe systems, albeit it is seldom used nowadays. In contrast to hierarchical models, which only allowed one parent-child relationship, network models broadened this to include numerous parent-child relationships. In 1969, a network data model definition was approved by the Conference on Data Systems Languages, often known as CODASYL, a defunct technical standards body. Thus, the network approach is also called the CODASYL model.

Relational data modelling

The relational data model was developed as an alternative to hierarchical and network models. The relational model, first outlined in a technical article by Edgar F. Codd of IBM in 1970, charts the connections between pieces of information kept in separate tables. The widespread use of relational databases in the 1980s and 1990s made relational modelling the de facto standard in data modelling by the mid-1990s.

Entity-relationship data modelling

Entity-relationship (ER) models are a specialised subset of the relational model that may be applied to non-relational databases. These models provide a graphical representation of entities, their properties, and their connections. ER models are ideal for transaction processing applications because of their streamlined data acquisition and updating approach. For instance, a data object on an employee may include fields for their name, date of birth, number of years worked there, and other information.

Dimensional data modelling

Data warehouses and data marts are common places to see dimensional data models in use since they provide the foundation for a wide variety of business intelligence tools. Dimension tables list characteristics of the entities in the fact tables, whereas fact tables provide data on transactions or other occurrences. A fact table may record the number of units sold to each customer, while related dimension tables may store information about the items and consumers. Examples of dimensional models include star schemas and snowflake schemas, both of which use numerous layers of dimension tables and link a fact table to various other tables.

Object-Oriented Data Modeling (ODM)

During the 1990s, the field of object-oriented programming flourished, and software companies began creating object databases, paving the way for the development of object-oriented data modelling. Unfortunately, object-oriented modelling hasn't gained widespread adoption since object databases are still specialised tools for a few uses. The ER and object-oriented approaches use representations of data, characteristics, and relationships, but the latter abstracts entities into objects. Classes are a way to organise things into groups based on their shared characteristics and behaviours; new classes may "inherit" the characteristics and behaviours of preexisting classes.

Graph data modelling

The graph data model evolved from the network and hierarchical models over the last several decades. The term is typically used in conjunction with graph databases to represent data sets having intricate connections between their elements. Graph data modelling, for instance, is often used in various recommendation engines and fraud detection software. One frequent category of data models is the property graph, in which "nodes" (representing data items and their associated attributes) are linked together by "edges" (representing relationships) to specify the nature of the connections between them.

Data modelling process

A company's information demands can't be met if data models don't adequately represent the business context of the data. During the conceptual and logical modelling stages, input from corporate leaders and employees is particularly crucial. Members of the data management team and the end consumers of the data should work together sequentially to construct the conceptual, logical, and physical data models.

A data modeller or data architect would often start a modelling project by conducting interviews with key business stakeholders to learn about the project's needs and to get insight into the organisation's operations. Conceptual and logical models may also get input from business analysts. In the latter stages of a project, the physical data model is utilised to convey technical specifications to database architects.

According to Peter Aiken, a data management consultant and associate professor of information systems at Virginia

Commonwealth University, the following six phases are recommended for building a data model.

1. Figure out what kinds of organisations are reflected in the data.
2. Differentiate between entities by determining their distinguishing features.
3. Firstly, you should sketch up an entity-relationship model to illustrate the relationships between your entities.
4. Figure out which characteristics of the data must be modelled.
5. Assigning characteristics to entities is a great way to see the business value of data.
6. Complete and verify the data model's correctness.

However, that's usually not the end; as an organisation's data assets and operational requirements evolve, data models will likely need to be updated and improved.

Essentials of data modelling

Effective data models are crucial to creating a strategy to maximise a company's data resources. Data modelling is useful for ensuring that databases and applications include relevant information and are built to accommodate organisational needs for data processing and administration.

The following are some additional advantages of data modelling:

- Convergence on data standards and definitions throughout the organisation. Data modelling aids in achieving enterprise-wide uniformity in data definitions, vocabulary, ideas, and forms.
- The growing participation of business users in data management. Due to the need for business input, data modelling fosters cooperation between data

management teams and business stakeholders, ultimately leading to enhanced systems.

- A better, cheaper database layout is possible. Data modelling helps database designers save time and effort by providing a clear blueprint they can follow while creating databases.
- Increased efficiency in using data resources. Improved corporate performance, more business prospects, and a competitive edge over competing organisations may all result from better data modelling.

Data modelling, however, is a complex process that is not always easy to implement. Some typical problems that might derail data modelling efforts are as follows:

- *The absence of organisational dedication and management support:* Achieving the necessary degree of company engagement is challenging if corporate and business leaders aren't convinced of the need for data modelling. This implies that executive buy-in for data management initiatives must be secured upfront.
- *Users in the corporate world don't get it*: Data modelling is an abstract process that may be hard for individuals to comprehend, even if business stakeholders are completely dedicated to it. To prevent this from happening, conceptual and logical data models must be grounded in common business ideas and jargon.
- *Complexity and creep in models:* Because of the size and complexity of data models, modelling projects may quickly become unmanageable if teams keep developing different versions of the models without settling on a final design. It's crucial to establish priorities and maintain a realistic project scope.
- *Lack of clarity or definition in the business needs:* Especially in the case of novel applications, the commercial side often lacks a well-defined set of data

requirements. Data modellers typically need to ask a series of questions to collect or clarify requirements and find the relevant data.

Techniques to use for data modelling

Several techniques can be used for data modelling, including:

Regression: This statistical technique is used to model the relationship between a dependent variable and one or more independent variables. It is often used to predict future outcomes based on past data.

Classification: This is a machine learning technique used to predict a categorical response based on one or more predictor variables. It is often used to assign data points to predefined categories or classes.

Clustering: This technique is used to group data points into clusters based on their similarities. It is often used to identify patterns and trends within a dataset.

Decision trees: This technique creates a tree-like model of decisions and their possible consequences based on certain conditions. It is often used for classification and prediction tasks.

Neural networks: This is a machine learning model inspired by the structure and function of the human brain. It is often used for complex tasks such as image or speech recognition.

Support vector machines (SVMs): This technique is used for classification and regression tasks. It works by finding the hyperplane in a high-dimensional space that maximally separates the different classes.

In fact, the choice of technique for data modelling will depend on the problem being solved and the characteristics of the data. Data scientists may need to try several different techniques and evaluate their performance in order to identify the best model for a given dataset.

Technologies to use for data modelling

Many different technologies can be used for data modelling, including:

Statistical software: There are many statistical software packages available that can be used for data modellings, such as R, SAS, SPSS, and STATA. These tools typically offer a wide range of statistical and machine-learning techniques for modelling data.

Machine learning libraries: There are many machine learning libraries available for programming languages, such as Python, including scikit-learn, TensorFlow, and Keras. These libraries provide a wide range of algorithms and tools for data modelling, including regression, classification, clustering, and neural networks.

Data visualisation tools: Data visualisation tools such as Tableau and QlikView can be used to create interactive visualisations of data, which can be useful for exploring and understanding data relationships and patterns.

Database management systems: Database management systems such as MySQL and MongoDB can store and manage large datasets and provide tools for querying and analysing data.

The choice of technology for data modelling will depend on the specific problem being solved and the characteristics of the data. Data scientists may need different technologies to model and analyse their data effectively.

Data Wrangling

Data wrangling, also known as data preparation or munging, is the cleaning, organising, and transforming of raw data into a usable form for analysis. This can involve tasks such as:

- Removing or correcting errors or inconsistencies in the data
- Handling missing or null values
- Combining or reshaping data from multiple sources
- Converting data into a format that can be easily analysed or visualised

Data wrangling is an important step in the data science process, as it can help ensure that the data is accurate and ready for analysis. It can be a time-consuming and labour-intensive process, especially when working with large or complex datasets.

Many tools and technologies are available for data wrangling, including programming languages such as Python and R, as well as specialized data wrangling software such as Open-Refine. Data wrangling often involves using these tools and techniques to clean and transform data effectively.

Data wrangling is a crucial step in the data science process, as it helps ensure that the data is ready for analysis and can provide accurate and valuable insights.

How does data wrangling work?

Data wrangling involves a series of steps to clean, organise, and transform raw data into a usable form for analysis. These steps can vary depending on the specific characteristics and needs of the data, but a typical data-wrangling process might include the following:

Data acquisition: This involves obtaining the raw data from a variety of sources, such as databases, flat files, or web APIs.

The data may be in a variety of formats, such as CSV, Excel, or JSON.

Data inspection: This involves examining the data to identify any errors, inconsistencies, or missing values. This can be done visually, using data visualisation tools, or programmatically, using programming languages such as Python or R.

Data cleaning: This involves correcting errors or inconsistencies in the data and handling missing or null values. This can involve a range of techniques, such as imputing missing values, dropping outliers, or standardising data formats.

Data transformation: This involves reshaping or combining data from multiple sources or converting the data into a format that can be easily analysed or visualised. This can involve tasks such as merging datasets, aggregating data or creating new features or variables.

Data storage: This involves storing the cleaned and transformed data in a suitable format and location for further analysis. This can involve storing the data in a database, flat file, or cloud storage solution.

Data wrangling is a process of cleaning, organising, and transforming raw data into a usable form for analysis. It can involve a range of techniques and tools, and it is an important step in the data science process to ensure that the data is ready for further analysis and can provide accurate and valuable insights.

Benefits of data wrangling

The data-wrangling procedure may take up to 80% of a data scientist's work. The issue "Is Data Wrangling worth the effort?" arises since only 20% of the budget goes into investigation and marketing. If you want to reap the numerous rewards that Data Wrangling offers, you should make an effort.

The advantages of using Data Wrangling for your company include the following:

Quite a Straightforward Dissection: Having cleaned and processed the raw data, Business analysts and stakeholders may now easily and quickly analyse even the most complicated data.

Simple data handling: Data Wrangling is the process of cleaning and organising raw data so that it may be used in analytical applications. Furthermore, the method enhances the data's quality, allowing for greater insight and use.

Improved targetting: Ads and content may be targeted more precisely when several data sets are combined in order to have a deeper understanding of the audience. Whether you're using Webinars to introduce your business to potential clients or an online learning platform to create a training programme for your staff, knowing your audience is essential to your success.

Efficient Use of Time: The Data Wrangling method frees analysts from the tedious task of trying to make sense of chaotic data, allowing them to focus instead on gaining insights from the data that will enable them to make educated judgements.

Clear visualisation: Data Clarity Through Exporting the cleaned and organised data to your preferred Analytics Visual Platform, you can immediately begin summarising, organising, and analysing the gathered information.

Data usability: Data wrangling enhances data usability by reformatting information so that the target application can read it.

Intuitive user interface: It helps with scheduling and automating the data flow process, making it easier to create data flows quickly and efficiently through an intuitive user interface.

Process lots of data: Data wrangling is the process of bringing together disparate data sets from many locations (databases, files, online services, etc.) to get insight into a problem. Users may simply exchange data flow methods and handle massive amounts of data using data wrangling.

Cost efficiency: It can help decrease expenditure variables from utilising non-essential software platforms or external APIs.

Data wrangling activities

Below, we will look at the six-step process for data wrangling, which includes everything required to make raw data usable.

Figure 44 - Data wrangling tasks

Data discovery

One of the broadest meanings of "data literacy" is learning how to use your information. Discovery is the initial phase of the data-wrangling process. A review of the information at hand is required, as is some consideration of how best to file and arrange it for ease of use.

So, you start with a chaotic mass of data gathered from various places and presented differently. To discover patterns and trends in the data, it is necessary first to collect all the disparate, siloed sources and set them up for analysis.

Data structuring

When first gathered, raw data may come in various shapes and sizes. There is no clear framework for it to follow. Thus, it is in disarray and devoid of any organisation. There must be some reorganisation to conform to the analytical model used by your company, which will also help with the analysis.

Most unstructured data consists of free-form language, although it may include numerical or identifying information. In this step of Data Wrangling, the dataset is parsed.

This procedure aims to glean helpful information from newly collected data. For instance, if you are working with code scraped from a website, you may need to parse the HTML code to extract the relevant parts and reject the rest.

The resulting spreadsheet will be more conducive to user interaction by adding columns, classes, headers, etc.

Data cleaning

Data Wrangling and Data Cleaning are sometimes used interchangeably but have different meanings. Of course, they aren't the same procedures at all. Cleaning is a complicated process in and of itself and is just one part of the more extensive data-wrangling process.

Algorithms are used to clean and organise the data. Typically, raw data has several inaccuracies that must be rectified before the data may go to the next phase. Outliers, errors, and bad data must all be corrected or deleted entirely throughout the data cleaning process.

The following are the effects of cleaning data:
- It filters out data points that are very unusual or rare, eliminating any chance of bias in subsequent analyses.
- Any blanks are filled in, and the data structure is standardised, making for more reliable results.
- Data duplication is found and eliminated, measuring techniques are standardised, typos and other structural problems are corrected, and the data is validated.

- Python and R are only two of the many programming languages that may be used to automate computational operations (more on that later).

Data enriching

By now, thanks to the data-wrangling process, you should know your way around the data and have a firm grasp on what it's all about.

The decision now is whether or not you want to lie or add to the information. Do you need it to be supplemented with other information?

You may increase the reliability of your research by combining your raw data with data from other sources, such as internal systems, third-party suppliers, etc. Your focus might also be on completing incomplete records. To illustrate, say that you want to merge two client information databases, but one has been addressed, and the other doesn't.

Data enrichment is a step you may take if your existing data falls short of your needs.

Data validation

If your data has quality problems, you can fix them with the right transformations, and that's what data validation is for.

Rules for data validation need iterative programming procedures to ensure the following.

- Quality vs Consistency
- Accuracy
- Security vs Authenticity

The fields in the datasets are validated, and the attribute distribution is determined to be normal, among other things. Attributes of the data are compared to predetermined rules using pre-programmed scripts.

Validation is the cornerstone of data cleaning and wrangling, and this case exemplifies the interaction between the two processes. Inevitably, you will uncover flaws in this procedure; therefore, you may need to do it more than once.

Data publishing

All the necessary procedures have been finished, and now the data is ready to be analysed. The last step is to make the Wrangled Data publicly available so that you and other interested parties may utilise it.

All the information may be transferred to a fresh system or database. Providing you followed all the previous steps properly, you should end up with high-quality data that can be used for all sorts of analytical and reporting purposes.

It's possible that you'll do further processing on the data to construct even more involved data structures, such as Data Warehouses. Now, anything may happen.

Data Visualisation

The term "data visualisation" refers to visually displaying data or information. Data visualisation tools make it easy to spot and comprehend anomalies, patterns, and trends in data using graphical representations such as charts, graphs, and maps.

Data visualisation tools and technologies are crucial in big data for sifting through mountains of data and arriving at well-informed conclusions. All aspects of modern society, from paintings and commercials to television and movies, rely heavily on visuals, and the human eye naturally attracts bright colours and intricate patterns. This truth needs to inform how we engage with data.

Objectives of data visualisation

It's crucial to remember that data visualisation isn't only for the data teams; it can be used for a wide range of applications. Data analysts and data scientists use it to find patterns and explain trends, while management uses it to portray organisational structure and hierarchy. Data visualisation may be used for many different things, but Harvard Business[11] identifies four main uses: ideation, illustration, discovery, and daily use. Below, we'll discuss them in further detail:

Idea generation

Data visualisation is often used as a group brainstorming tool. They are often used at the outset of a project, during brainstorming or Design Thinking sessions, to help gather ideas from a variety of people and then emphasise the group's shared problems. While these visualisations are often rough around the edges, they provide the groundwork for the project and help the team focus on what has to be done to solve the issue that matters to the stakeholders.

Idea illustration

Concepts, such as strategies and procedures, may be more easily communicated via data visualisation for concept representation. Its most popular use is in educational contexts, including tutorials, certification programmes, and centres of excellence; it may also be used to illustrate organisational structures and procedures to improve communication amongst the appropriate people working on a given project. Gantt charts and waterfall charts are common tools for project managers to use to visualise processes. Data modelling also simplifies developers, business analysts, data architects, and others to comprehend the connections in a database or data warehouse by using abstraction to depict and better understand data flow inside an enterprise's information system.

Visual discovery

Data teams are more suited to visual discovery, and routine data visualisation practises. Everyday data viz enables the following narrative when a new insight has been uncovered. In contrast, visual discovery aids data analysts, data scientists, and other data professionals in identifying patterns and trends within a dataset.

Information Display

Data visualisation is essential to the data science process for better communication with coworkers and decision-makers. Reporting system management teams often resort to pre-made template views to keep an eye on things. Visualisation isn't only for performance dashboards, however. In text mining, for instance, an analyst may utilise a word cloud to quickly grasp overarching themes, patterns, and connections in large amounts of unstructured data. They might use a graph representation instead to show the connections between nodes in a knowledge network. It's vital to remember that the ability to express data in various formats is a talent that must be shared outside your core analytics team.

Types of data visualisation

Many different types of data visualisations can be used, including:

Line graphs: These are used to show trends over time or to compare multiple data series.

Bar charts: These are used to compare categorical or numerical data.

Histograms: These are used to show the distribution of numerical data.

Scatter plots: These are used to visualise the relationship between two numerical variables.

Pie charts: These are used to show the proportions of a whole.

Heat maps: These are used to visualise the intensity of a variable across two dimensions.

Box plots: These are used to show the distribution of numerical data and identify outliers.

Choropleth maps: These are used to visualise spatial data and show the distribution of a variable across a geographic region.

Treemaps: These are used to visualise hierarchical data and show the proportion of each subcategory within a larger category.

As a matter of fact, the choice of data visualisation will depend on the specific characteristics and needs of the data and the goals of the analysis. Data scientists may need to try several visualisations to effectively communicate the insights and trends in the data.

Open-source visualisation tools

Access to data visualisation tools has never been easier. Open-source libraries, such as D3.js, allow analysts to present data interactively and engage a broader audience with new data. Some of the most popular open-source visualisation libraries include:

D3.js: It is a front-end JavaScript library for producing dynamic, interactive data visualisations in web browsers. D3.js (link resides outside IBM) uses HTML, CSS, and SVG to create visual representations of data that can be viewed on any browser. It also provides features for interactions and animations.

ECharts: A powerful charting and visualisation library that offers an easy way to add intuitive, interactive, and highly customizable charts to products, research papers, presentations, etc. Echarts (link resides outside IBM) is based on JavaScript and ZRender, a lightweight canvas library.

Vega: Vega (link resides outside IBM) defines itself as "visualisation grammar," providing support to customize visualisations across large datasets accessible from the web.

deck.gl: It is part of Uber's open-source visualisation framework suite. deck.gl (link resides outside IBM) is a framework used for exploratory data analysis on big data. It helps build high-performance GPU-powered visualisation on the web.

Data visualisation tools

The appropriate software can help you visualise information for your data stories.

Here are some of the free data visualisation tools:

G-Suite: You can use Google Sheets for plotting, and Google Slides for annotation. In addition, Google Data Studio offers useful features for time series visualisation and integrates with Google Analytics.

Microsoft Power BI: This software allows you to unify data from many sources to create interactive and immersive dashboards or reports.

Leaflet: This open-source JavaScript library can be incorporated into your data visualisation framework for building interactive maps.

Tableau Public: You can download the full version of this software for free, under the condition that everything you create with the tool is made public through Tableau Gallery.

Datawrapper: The same tool journalists use in leading publications, this software allows you to create charts, maps and tables from complex datasets.

Open Refine: This platform goes beyond data visualisation by cleaning and transforming data and extending it with web services and external data.

Data visualisation categories

When considering the different types of data visualisation, it helps to be aware of the different categories that these visualisations may fall into:

Temporal data visualisations are linear and one-dimensional. Examples include scatterplots, timelines, and line graphs.

Hierarchical visualisations organise groups within larger groups and are often used to display clusters of information. Examples include tree diagrams, ring charts, and sunburst diagrams.

Network visualisation shows the relationships and connections between multiple datasets. Examples include matrix charts, word clouds, and node-link diagrams.

Multidimensional or 3D visualisations are used to depict two or more variables. Examples include pie charts, Venn diagrams, stacked bar graphs, and histograms.

Geospatial visualisations convey various data points in relation to physical, real-world locations (for example, voting patterns across a certain country). Examples include heat maps, cartograms, and density maps.

Data visualisation techniques

Many techniques can be used in visualisation to communicate data trends, patterns, and relationships effectively. Some of the most common techniques include:

Filtering: This involves selecting a subset of the data to display in the visualisation in order to focus on specific trends or patterns.

Grouping: This involves dividing the data into categories or groups and visualising the data separately for each group.

Aggregation: This involves summarising the data using statistical measures such as mean, median, or mode and visualising the summary statistics.

Encoding: This involves visual elements such as position, size, colour, or shape to represent different variables or data values in the visualisation.

Annotation: This involves adding labels or notes to the visualisation to provide context or clarify the meaning of the data.

Layout: This involves organizing the visual elements in the visualisation to communicate the data and highlight important trends or patterns effectively.

As I mentioned earlier, the choice of technique will depend on the specific characteristics and needs of the data, as well as the goals of the analysis. Data scientists may need to use a combination of different techniques to communicate the insights and trends in the data effectively.

Mathematical Data Science

Mathematics is a fundamental part of data science, providing the tools and techniques for analysing, modelling, and understanding data. There are many different areas of mathematics that are important for data science, including:

Linear algebra: This is the study of vectors and matrices and is used for tasks such as matrix operations, data manipulation, and dimensionality reduction.

Calculus: This is the study of rates of change and optimisation and is used for tasks such as gradient descent, optimisation, and curve fitting.

Probability: This is the study of random events and their outcomes and is used for tasks such as modelling uncertainty, making predictions, and identifying patterns in data.

Statistics: This is the study of collecting, analyzing, and interpreting data and is used for hypothesis testing, inference, and model evaluation.

Optimisation: This is the study of finding the best solution to a problem and is used for tasks such as feature selection, model selection, and hyperparameter tuning.

Mathematics is essential to data science, as it provides the tools and techniques for understanding and analyzing data. Data scientists need to have a strong foundation in mathematics to work with data and draw meaningful insights from it effectively.

Linear algebra

Linear algebra is a branch of mathematics that deals with linear equations and their representations in vector spaces. It is a fundamental mathematical tool used in many sciences, engineering, and mathematics areas, including data science.

In data science, linear algebra is used in a variety of ways, including:

Matrix operations: Matrices are a fundamental data structure in linear algebra and are widely used in data science to represent and manipulate data. Matrix operations, such as addition, multiplication, and transposition, can be used to perform tasks such as data transformation, aggregation, and feature scaling.

Linear regression: Linear regression is a statistical technique used to model the relationship between a dependent variable and one or more independent variables. It is based on the assumption that the relationship between the variables is linear, and it uses linear algebra to find the line of best fit.

Dimensionality reduction: Many data sets have many features or dimensions, making it difficult to analyse and interpret the data. Linear algebra techniques such as singular value decomposition (SVD) and principal component analysis (PCA) can reduce the data's dimensionality and make it more manageable.

Example of linear algebra

Suppose you have a dataset with two features, X and Y, and you want to use linear regression to model the relationship between these variables. You can represent the dataset as a matrix, where each row represents a data point, and each column represents a feature.

For example, the matrix might look like this:

[X1 Y1]
[X2 Y2]
[X3 Y3]
...

To perform linear regression, you need to find the line of best fit that describes the relationship between X and Y. This line is represented by a linear equation of the form $Y = mX + b$, where m is the slope of the line and b is the y-intercept.

To find the optimal values of m and b, you can use linear algebra to solve a system of linear equations. This involves finding the values of m and b that minimise the sum of the squared errors between the predicted values of Y (based on the equation) and the actual values of Y in the dataset.

This is just a simple example of how linear algebra can be used in data science, but there are many other applications as well. Linear algebra is a powerful tool that is essential for working with data in data science.

Calculus

Calculus is a branch of mathematics that deals with the study of change and motion. It is used to model and analyse problems involving rates of change, optimisation, and the accumulation of quantities.

In data science, calculus is used in a variety of ways, including:

Optimisation: Calculus is used to find the optimal values of parameters or variables in a given problem. For example, in machine learning, calculus can be used to find the values of weights and biases in a neural network that minimises the loss function.

Derivatives: Derivatives are used to measure the rate of change of a function, and they play a key role in optimisation problems. In data science, derivatives are used to optimise the performance of machine learning algorithms and analyse function behaviour.

Integrals: Integrals are used to calculate the accumulated value of a function over a given range. In data science, integrals can be used to perform tasks such as calculating the area under a curve or estimating the probability of a given event.

Differential equations: Differential equations are used to model problems involving rates of change and motion. In data science, differential equations are used to model and analyse systems of interacting variables, such as in the analysis of time series data or the modelling of complex systems.

Example of calculus

Suppose you are training a machine learning model to predict the price of a stock based on its historical data. To optimise the model's performance, you need to find the values of the weights and biases that minimise the difference between the predicted and actual stock prices.

To do this, you can use calculus to calculate the derivative of the loss function (which measures the difference between the predicted and actual stock prices) concerning the weights and biases. The derivative tells you how the loss function changes as the weights and biases change, and it can be used to find the optimal values that minimise the loss.

Calculus enables data scientists to perform various tasks, from optimisation and analysis to modelling and prediction.

Probability

Please see the section on "Statistical Concepts of Data Science."

Example of probability

Suppose you are working on a machine learning project to predict whether customers will churn (cancel their subscription) based on their past behaviour. Your dataset includes customer usage patterns, demographics, and other factors.

To make predictions about churn, you can use probability to calculate the likelihood that a given customer will churn based on their past behaviour. For example, you might calculate the probability that a customer will churn based on their usage patterns (e.g., how often they log in, how much they use the service, etc.). You can then use this probability to classify the customer as likely to churn or not likely to churn.

Statistics

Please see the section on "Statistical Concepts of Data Science."

Example of statistics

Suppose you are working on a project to predict the demand for a product based on past sales data. You have a dataset that includes information about the product's sales over time and other factors that might influence demand (e.g., price, advertising, seasonality, etc.).

To make predictions about demand, you can use statistical techniques to analyse the data and identify patterns and trends. For example, you might use statistical tests to determine whether the sales of the product are correlated with certain factors (e.g., price, seasonality, etc.), or you might use statistical models (such as linear regression) to fit a curve to the data and make predictions about future demand.

Discrete mathematics

Discrete mathematics is a branch of mathematics that deals with discrete objects, such as integers, graphs, and logic statements. It is a fundamental mathematical tool in many sciences, engineering, and computer science areas, including data science.

In data science, discrete mathematics is used in a variety of ways, including:

Combinatorics: Combinatorics is the study of combinations and arrangements of objects. In data science, combinatorics counts the possible outcomes or configurations of a given problem.

Graph theory: Graph theory studies graphs and mathematical structures used to model relationships between objects. In data science, graph theory analyses and understands complex networks, such as social networks or web graphs.

Set theory: Set theory studies sets, which are collections of objects. In data science, set theory represents and manipulates data and performs tasks such as data aggregation and grouping.

Logic: Logic is the study of reasoning and argumentation. In data science, logic is used to represent and manipulate data and perform tasks such as data validation and reasoning about uncertain events.

Discrete maths enables data scientists to perform a wide range of tasks, from data manipulation and analysis to modelling and prediction.

Algorithms

Algorithms are sets of instructions or rules used to solve problems or accomplish tasks. In data science, algorithms are used to analyse and process data in order to extract insights, make predictions, or perform other useful operations.

There are many different types of algorithms used in data science, including:

Machine learning algorithms: Machine learning algorithms are a type of algorithm that can learn from data and improve their performance over time. They are used to build predictive models, classify data, and perform other tasks.

Data mining algorithms: Data mining algorithms are used to extract useful patterns and trends from large datasets. They are used to discover insights that can inform business decisions or scientific research.

Optimisation algorithms: Optimisation algorithms are used to find the optimal solution to a given problem. They are used to optimise machine learning models' performance and solve other optimisation problems.

Search algorithms: Search algorithms are used to find specific items or solutions in a dataset. They are used to perform tasks such as searching through a database or finding the shortest path between two points.

Algorithms are a critical tool in data science, as they enable data scientists to analyse and process data in order to extract useful insights and make informed decisions.

Algorithm example

Suppose you are working on a project to predict the likelihood that a customer will churn (cancel their subscription) based on their past behaviour. Your dataset includes customer usage patterns, demographics, and other factors.

To make predictions about churn, you can use a machine learning algorithm such as a decision tree or a random forest. These algorithms use the data to learn patterns and relationships that can be used to predict churn. For example, the algorithm might learn that customers who log in less frequently are more likely to churn or that younger customers are less likely to churn.

You would first split the data into training and test sets to build the model. The algorithm would then be trained on the training set, using the data to learn patterns and relationships. Once the model has been trained, you can use it to make predictions on the test set, and you can evaluate the accuracy of the predictions to determine how well the model is performing.

Big Data

We must first look at the historical background to properly understand big data. According to Gartner's 2001 definition (which is still widely used), big data is a variety of data pouring out at an unprecedented rate. It is called the so-called 3V of Velocity, Volume, and Variety.

In simple terms, big data can be described as a more complex and more extensive dataset collected from new data sources. These data sets are enormous and challenging to manage with traditional data processing software. However, with this massive amount of data, you can solve many business-related problems that were previously not solved.

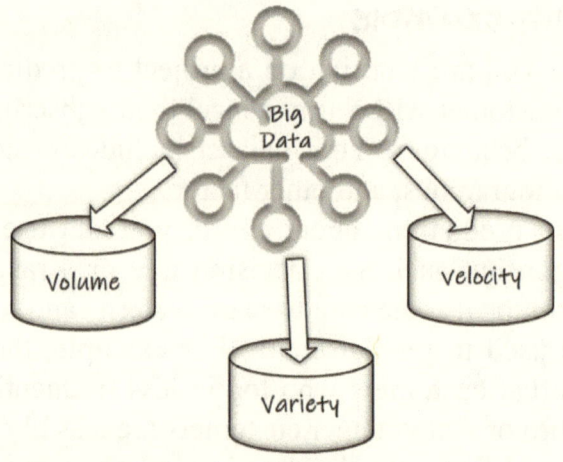

Figure 45 - The three dimensions of the Big Data

Big Data 3V

Velocity	In big data, speed refers to the speed at which data is received or (maybe) processed. Normally, it is fastest when data is streamed directly to memory

	than when it is written to disk. Some internet-based smart products operate at real-time or near-real-time speeds, requiring real-time evaluation and operation.
Volume	The amount of data matters. It can be tens of terabytes of data for some organisations and hundreds of petabytes of data for others. Examples include data of unknown value, such as Twitter data feed, click trends on webpages or mobile apps, and data collected from sensor-based devices. Dealing with big data means dealing with low-density, unstructured data in large volumes.
Variety	In big data, diversity means countless types of data available. It is structured and structured data for existing data types, which fits exactly into relational databases. However, with the advent of big data, new types of unstructured data are being created. Semi-structured and unstructured data such as text, audio, and video require additional pre-processing to derive their meaning and support the metadata.

Table 2 - The Three Vs of Big Data

The Value and Truth of Big Data

Over the past two years, V has appeared more, just 'value (Value)' and 'accuracy (Veracity)'.

Data has its own value. However, it is useless unless you discover these values. Another important point to note is, 'How authentic and reliable is the data we hold?'

Looking at the world's largest tech companies, much of the value they provide comes from data, which continuously analyses this data to increase efficiency and develop new products.

Recent innovations have dramatically reduced data storage and computing costs, making it easier to store more significant amounts of data at a lower cost than ever before. Business decisions have been made more accurately, as large volumes of big data are more affordable and easily accessible.

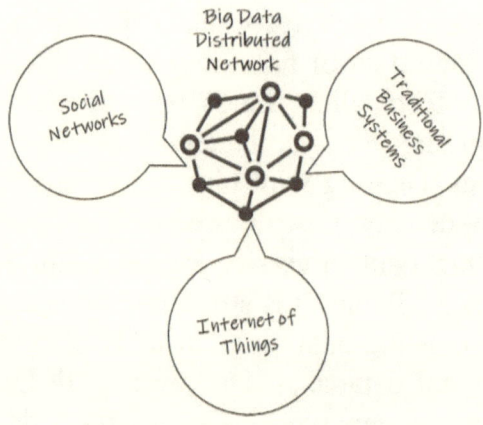

Figure 46 - Big Data Capture Networks

Finding value in big data isn't just about analysing data (of course, it has benefits as well). Analysts, business users, and corporate executives can ask appropriate questions, read patterns, make information-based assumptions, and predict behaviour to carry out this process. This is the whole process of deriving value.

Big Data History

The concept of big data itself is relatively new, but the origins of large data sets date back to the 1960s and 1970s when the world of data was just beginning to open as the first data centres were established and relational databases were developed.

Then, as we entered 2005, people began to realise that there were thousands of data users arising from online services such as Facebook and YouTube. That same year Hadoop (an open-source framework created for storing and analysing big data sets) emerged. During this time, NoSQL also began to gain popularity.

The development of open-source frameworks like Hadoop (and, more recently, Spark) has played an essential role in the growth of big data. This is because an open-source framework makes big data easier and lowers storage costs. Since then, the volume of big data has been growing exponentially. Users are still generating massive amounts of data, but it's not just humans who create it.

With the advent of the Internet of Things (IoT), many objects and devices are connected to the Internet, collecting data on customer usage patterns and product performance. With the advent of Machine Learning, the amount of data has increased.

In this way, big data has evolved, but big data's usefulness is still a taste. Cloud computing is expanding the potential of big data more than ever. The cloud offers flexible scalability, so developers can leverage ad hoc clusters to test subsets of data.

Big Data and Data Analytics Benefits

Big data provides more information so that you can get more complete answers. A more comprehensive response means more confidence in your data and a new approach to problem-solving.

Big Data Use Cases

Big data helps you handle many business activities, from customer experience to analytics.

Product Development

Companies like Netflix and Procter & Gamble (P&G) use big data to predict customer needs ahead of time. They are building predictive models for developing new products/services by classifying key attributes of previous and current products/services and modelling the relationship between them and the product/service's commercial success. In particular, P&G uses data and analysis results from focus groups, SNS, test markets, and initial store launch product performances for new product planning, production, and launch.

Forecast-based Maintenance

Factors that can predict equipment failures can be hidden deep within unstructured data that encompasses millions of log entries, sensor data, error messages, engine temperature, and more, in addition to structured data such as the machine year, manufacturer, and machine model. Companies can cost-effectively perform maintenance while maximising component and equipment uptime by analysing the factors that suggest potential problems before they occur.

Customer Experience (CX)

The competition to attract customers has begun. We are able to analyse the customer experience from a clearer perspective than ever before. With big data, you can improve the interaction environment and maximise value by collecting data from various sources such as SNS, web visit history, and call logs. Reduce customer churn and respond proactively to business-related issues by providing personalised service.

Fraud and Compliance

Security isn't just about fighting a handful of hackers; it's about fighting a group of professional hackers. The security context and compliance requirements are becoming increasingly demanding. Big data can help you identify patterns in your data that suggest a fraudulent activity, and large aggregate amounts of information create regulatory reports more quickly.

Machine Learning in Big Data

One of the drivers of the popularity of Machine Learning is data, massive data. Instead of programming machines, we can now teach ourselves. This is thanks to big data training Machine Learning models.

Operational efficiency

Operational efficiency isn't always an essential factor, but it's clear that big data is the most influential area. With big data, you can analyse and evaluate various factors such as production processes, customer feedback, and revenue to reduce problems and predict future requirements. It can also effectively make decisions regarding the current market demands.

The Driving Force of Innovation

Big data can enable innovation. This is because you can study the interdependence between people, institutions, companies, and processes and discover new ways to use the analytics you get. Use data analytics to make financial and planning decisions effectively. Research market trends and customer needs to provide new products and services. Implement dynamic pricing policies. There are endless possibilities for big data.

Big Data Problems

Big data has many benefits, but that doesn't mean it's all without problems.

First of all, it's big. Although new technologies have been developed for data storage, the amount of data doubles every two years. And companies, too, are still struggling to find ways to store their data to keep pace with this growth efficiently.

However, simply keeping the data is not enough. Data must be used with value, depending on how you curate it. A lot of work is required to classify or organise the data related to the customer to be analysed meaningfully. Data scientists spend 50-80% of their time curating and writing data before it is used.

Finally, big data technology is changing rapidly. A few years ago, Apache Hadoop was the most used for big data processing. Then, with the advent of Apache Spark in 2014, combining these two frameworks is considered the most efficient approach. There is an endless effort to keep pace with the trend of big data technology.

How Big Data Works

Big data provides new insights to create new opportunities and business models. In order to use big data in earnest, the following three core tasks must be preceded.

Integration: Big data collects and aggregates data from a variety of different types of sources and applications. Existing data integration mechanisms such as ETL (Extract, Transfer, Load) can never respond to big data. New strategies and technologies are required to analyse big data sets at terabytes or even petabytes.

During the integration process, the data must be fetched, processed, and configured in a format that business analysts can use.

Management: Big data needs storage. As a storage solution, you can choose either the cloud or on-premises or use both. You can archive your data in any format and then apply the processing requirements and process engines you need to your data sets on demand. Most people choose the right storage solution based on the data's location. Cloud solutions are becoming increasingly popular in that they support users' current computing needs and are free to use resources whenever needed.

Analysis: Investing in big data starts to shine the moment you analyse and put it into action. Improve data clarity with visual analysis of different kinds of data sets. Explore your data in-depth to discover new things. Share this information with others.

Build data models with Machine Learning and Artificial Intelligence technologies. Put your data to work.

Technologies and Trends in Working with Big Data

Initially, the approaches and technologies included tools for massively parallel processing of indefinitely structured data, such as NoSQL DBMS, MapReduce algorithms, and Hadoop project tools. In the future, other solutions that provide similar capabilities for processing ultra-large data arrays and some hardware will begin to be classified as big data technologies.

MapReduce: It is s a model of distributed parallel computing in computer clusters presented by Google. According to this model, the application is divided into many identical elementary tasks executed on the cluster nodes and then naturally reduced to the final result.

NoSQL: It is a general term for various non-relational databases and storages, and does not mean anyone-specific technology or product. Conventional relational databases are well suited for fairly fast and uniform queries, and on complex and flexible queries typical for big data, the load exceeds reasonable limits, and the use of the DBMS becomes ineffective.

Hadoop: It is a freely distributed set of utilities, libraries and framework for developing and executing distributed programs on clusters of hundreds and thousands of nodes. It is considered one of the foundational technologies of big data.

R: R is a programming language for statistical data processing and graphics. It is widely used for data analysis and has become the de-facto standard for statistical programs.

Hardware Solutions: Teradata corporations, EMC and others offer hardware and software systems designed for processing big data. These complexes are supplied as ready-to-install telecom cabinets containing a server cluster and control software for massively parallel processing. This also sometimes includes hardware solutions for analytical processing in RAM, in particular, Hana hardware and software systems from SAP and Exalytics[12] complex from Oracle, even though such processing is not initially massively parallel, and the amount of RAM of one node is limited to several terabytes.

Big Data Open-source Tools

Data analysis is a process of verifying, cleaning, transforming, and modelling data to discover useful information, offer, and make decisions. Thousands of big data tools are available to analyse the data today. Here are the top tools and resources for open-source data analysis, visualisation, extraction, and databases.

1. KNIME

The KNIME Analytics platform is a leading open-source solution for data-based innovation, helping you identify the potential hidden in your data, expand opportunities for new ideas, or predict new trends.

KNIME Analytics is the perfect toolkit for any research scientist, with more than 1,000 modules, hundreds of ready-to-run examples, a wide range of integrated tools, and advanced algorithms.

2. OpenRefine

OpenRefine (formerly Google Refine) is a powerful tool for dealing with unprepared data: cleaning it up, converting it from one format to another, and sniping it with web services. OpenRefine can help you easily explore Big Data.

3. R - the programming language

What if I told you that Project R, the GNU project, is written in R itself? It is primarily written on C and Fortran. And many of its modules are written in R. It's a free programming language and software environment for statistical computing and graphics. The R language is widely used for statistical software development and data analysis. The ease of use and scaling has greatly increased the popularity of R in recent years.

Data mining provides statistical and graphic methods, including linear and non-linear modelling, classical statistical tests, time-series analysis, classification, clustering, and others.

4. Orange

Orange is an open-source data visualisation and data analysis for beginners and experts and provides interactive workflows with a large set of Big Data tools. Orange contains various visualisations, from scattering charts, histograms, and trees to dendrograms, nets and heat maps.

5. RapidMiner

RapidMiner makes you more productive with an open-source platform to prepare data, machine learning, and deploy a model. Like KNIME, RapidMiner works through visual programming and is able to manipulate, analyse, and model data. Its unified data research platform accelerates the construction of complete analytical workflows, from data preparation to machine learning, from modelling to deployment, in a single environment, greatly increasing efficiency and reducing the time it takes to implement research projects.

6. Pentaho

Pentaho removes barriers that block your organisation's ability to gain value from all your data. The platform simplifies the preparation and mix of any data and includes a range of tools for easy analysis, visualisation, study, report and forecasting. The open, embedded, and expandable Pentaho is designed to ensure that everyone on your team can easily translate data into value from developers to business users.

7. Talend

Talend is a leading provider of open-source software to data-oriented enterprises. Our customers connect anywhere, at any speed. Talend is used in Big Data, 5 times faster and with a 1/5th cost.

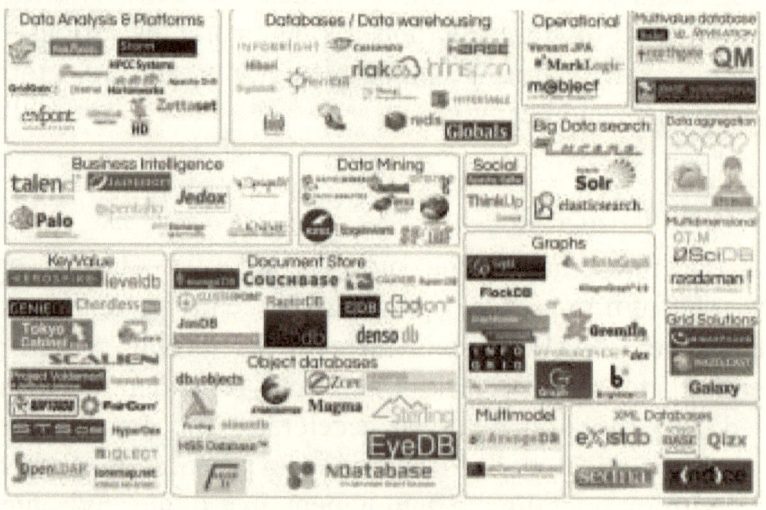

Figure 47 - Big data technology stack

8. Weka

Weka, an open-source software, is a suite of machine learning algorithms for data mining and Big Data tasks. Algorithms can be applied directly to the dataset or triggered from your own JAVA code. It's also good for developing new machine learning algorithms because it's fully implemented in the JAVA programming language and supports several standard data mining tasks.

For those unfamiliar with Java, Weka, with its GUI, provides the most effortless transition to the world of Data Science. Those with Java experience can also use the library in their code when written in Java.

9. NodeXL

NodeXL is software for visualising and analysing data from relationships and networks. NodeXL provides accurate calculations. It's free (non-professional) and open-source software analysis and visualisation. It is one of the best statistical tools for data analysis, including advanced network metrics, access to network data providers, and automation.

10. Gephi

Gephi is also an open-source analysis and visualisation software package written in Java on the NetBeans platform. Think of giant relationship maps that represent connected connections or Facebook friends. Gephi works in this direction by providing accurate calculations.

Big data tools for data visualisation

Here are some standard tools used for Big data visualisation.

11. Datawrapper

Datawrapper is a data visualisation tool for creating interactive graphs. Once you download data from the CSV/PDF/Excel file or insert it directly into the box, Datawrapper creates a bar, line, map, or other related visualisation. Datawrapper graphics can be built into any website or CMS through the insert code. A lot of news organisations use Datawrapper to embed live graphs into their articles. It is very easy to use and creates spectacular graphics.

12. Solver

Solver specialises in providing world-class financial reporting, budgeting, and button-access analysis to all data sources that ensure its profitability. Solver provides BI360, which is available for cloud and local deployment, focusing on four key analytics areas.

13. Qlik

You can create visualisations, dashboards, and apps that answer your company's most important questions. Now you can see the whole story that is in your data.

14. Tableau

Tableau simplifies visualisation in an elegant and intuitive tool. It is exceptionally effective in business because it transmits information through data visualisation. In the analytical process, Tableau's visual effects allow you to quickly investigate the hypothesis, test your hypothesis, or simply study the data before proceeding with a detailed analysis.

15. Google Fusion Tables

Google Fusion Tables are more advanced tables similar to Spreadsheets. Google Fusion Tables is an incredible tool for data analysis, big data visualisation and display. Unsurprisingly, Google's astonishing mapping software plays a big role in promoting this tool. Take, for example, this map to look at the oil production platforms in the Gulf of Mexico.

16. Infogram

Infogram offers more than 35 interactive maps and more than 500 maps to help you visualise your data beautifully. Create a variety of diagrams, including columns, bars, pie, or word clouds. You can even add a map to your infographic or report to really impress your audience.

Sentiment text analysis
17. Opentext

The Sentiment OpenText analysis module is a specialised classification mechanism used to identify and evaluate subjective patterns and expressions of feelings in the textual content. The analysis is done at the theme, proposal and document level and aims to determine whether parts of the text are factual or subjective, and in the latter case, if the opinion expressed in these parts of the content is positive, negative, mixed or neutral.

18. Semantria

Semantria is a tool that offers a unique service approach, collecting texts, tweets and other comments from customers and carefully analysing them to get practical and valuable ideas. Semantria offers text analysis through the API plugin and Excel. It differs from Lexalytics in that it is offered through the API plug-in and Excel, and it includes an extensive knowledge base and uses deep learning.

19. Trackur

Trackur's automatic sentiment analysis looks at the specific keyword you control and then determines whether the keyword's mood is positive, negative, or neutral. This is what sets Trackur apart from the rest. It can monitor all social networks and mainstream news, obtain information about managers through trends, search keywords, analyse moods with the automated sentiment, and assess influence.

20. SAS sentiment analysis

SAS sentiment analysis automatically extracts moods in real-time or over some time with a unique combination of statistical modelling and rule-based natural language processing methods. Built-in reports show samples and detailed reactions. With current assessments, you can improve models and categorise them to reflect emerging topics and new terms related to your customers, organisation, or industry.

21. Opinion Crawl

Opinion Crawl is an online sentiment analysis for current events, companies, products, and people. Opinion Crawl allows visitors to rate web sentiment on a topic - a person, an event, a company, or a product. You can enter the theme and get a special assessment. For each topic, you get a pie chart that shows current moods in real-time, a list of recent news headlines, a few smaller images, and a tag cloud of key semantic concepts that the public associates with the object. Concepts allow you to see which problems or events are feeling positive or negative. For a deeper assessment, web scanners will find the latest published content on many popular topics and current public issues and consider them to be in a constant mood. The blog posts will then show the trend of sentiment over time and the attitude of "Positive attitude to denial."

Big data extraction tools or parcels
22. Octoparse

Octoparse is a free and powerful tool that is used to extract almost all the data you need from a website. You can use Octoparse to copy the website with its extensive functionality. Its mouse-cursor user interface helps non-programmers quickly get used to Octoparse. This allows you to capture all text from the site using AJAX, JavaScript and, thus, you can download almost all of the site's content and save it in a structured format such as EXCEL, TXT, HTML or your databases.

23. Content Grabber

Content Graber is an enterprise-oriented online scanning software. It can extract content from almost any website and store it as structured data in your chosen format, including Excel, XML, CSV, and most databases. Users can use a C, or VB.NET, to debug or record a scenario to manage the bypass processing process. It's more suited to people with advanced programming skills because it offers many powerful scripted edits and debugs interfaces for people in need.

24. Import.io

Import.io is a web tool for extracting data that allows you to extract information from sites. Just highlight what you need, and Import.io will guide you and help you "learn" what you are looking for. Import.io will dig and extract data for analysis or export from there.

25. Parsehub

Parsehub is an excellent web boiler supporting data collection from websites using AJAX, JavaScript, cookies, etc. As free software, you can create no more than five projects for publication in Parsehub.

26. Mozenda

Mozenda is a web search service. It provides many valuable features for extracting data. Users will be allowed to upload the extracted data to the cloud.

27. Scraper

Scraper is a free web search tool that works right in your browser and automatically generates XPath to identify URLs. Scraper is a Chrome extension with limited data retrieval capabilities, but it's useful for online research and data exports to Google spreadsheets. This tool is designed for beginners and experts who can easily copy data into the clipboard or store it in OAuth spreadsheets.

Datasets or datasets in Big Data

Here are some datasets:

28. Data.gov

The U.S. government has promised to make all government data available on the Internet. This site is the first stage and acts as a portal for fantastic information about everything from climate to crime.

29. U.S. Census Bureau

The U.S. Census Bureau provides extensive information on the lives of U.S. citizens covering population data, geographic data, and education.

30. CIA World Newsletter

World Factbook provides information on history, people, government, economy, geography, communications, transportation, military and transnational issues for 267 global organisations.

31. PubMed

PubMed, developed by the National Library of Medicine (NLM), provides free access to MEDLINE, a database of more than 11 million bibliographic references and abstracts from nearly 4,500 journals in medicine, nursing, dentistry, veterinary medicine, pharmacy, health systems and preclinical sciences. PubMed also contains links to full-text versions of articles on the websites of participating publishers. In addition, PubMed provides access and links to integrated molecular biology databases supported by the National Centre for Biotechnology Information (NCBI). These databases contain DNA and protein sequences, 3-D protein structure data, population survey data sets and complete genomes assembly in an integrated system. PubMed adds additional NLM bibliographic databases, such as AIDSLINE. PubMed includes Old Medline. "Old Medline" covers 1950-1965. (Updated daily).

Best free online big data and data science courses

Coursera – Data Science Specialisation

Coursera – Data-Driven Decision Making
EdX – Data Science Essentials
Udacity – Intro to Machine Learning
IBM – Data Science Fundamentals
California Institute of Technology – Learning from Data
Dataquest – Become a Data Scientist
KDNuggets – Data Mining Course
The Open-Source Data Science Masters

Understanding Machine Learning

Machine Learning (ML) is positioned as a technology that forms the basis of Artificial Intelligence. However, data mining that analyses vast amounts of big data and technologies used for anomaly detection and predictive maintenance of factory equipment are fields overlapping with Machine Learning.

Machine Learning differs from data mining in that it takes the following action based on the presence or absence of data to be learned in advance and the learning result. To sort out the differences, data mining aims to mine unknown features from vast amounts of data. On the other hand, Machine Learning learns features from existing data to make predictions and inferences.

Machine Learning is considered a branch of Artificial Intelligence because the main idea is that the computer does not just use a pre-written algorithm but learns to solve the problem.

Machine Learning takes an increasing place in our daily life due to the vast range of its applications. From traffic analysis to self-driving cars, more and more tasks are shifted to self-learning vehicles.

Any working Machine Learning technology can be conditionally attributed to one of three levels of availability

Machine Learning is now at the junction of the second and third levels, due to which the rate of change in the world with the help of this technology is growing every day.

What is ML?

You may be wondering, "Is the computer mechanical?" Machine Learning is literally "learning mechanically." In short, "learning repeatedly and repeatedly" is called Machine Learning.

Computers, called Artificial Intelligence, do not have this kind of performance when they are programmed. Then, the reason why Artificial Intelligence is active these days is born is that developers take in innumerable data and repeat learning. That technique and work are called Machine Learning.

On the other hand, Deep Learning is a type of Machine Learning, but it further develops that technology. Deep Learning is "learning with a thinking circuit closer to humans." A "neural network" circuit that artificially imitates a human neural circuit is used to create advanced Artificial Intelligence.

Machine Learning algorithms

An "algorithm" is a calculation method used on a computer. And there are various algorithms in the computer world, and the appropriate one depends on the purpose. In Machine Learning, in order to learn data efficiently, it is common to use an algorithm suitable for it. This algorithm can be broadly classified into the following five categories.

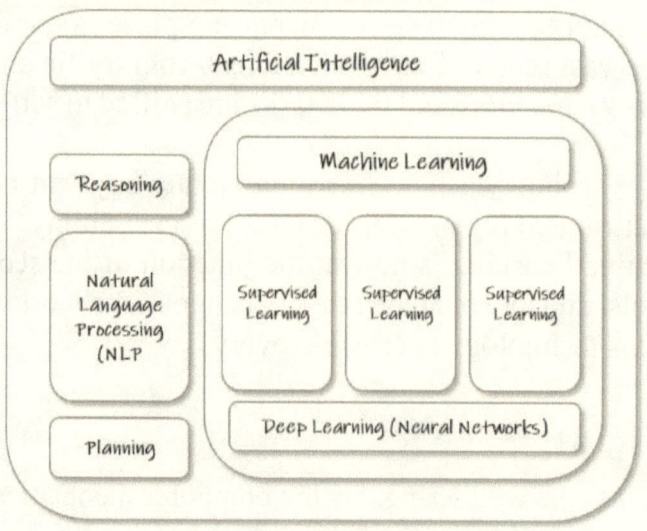

Figure 48 – AI, ML DL Relationships

Classification (supervised learning)

The basic algorithm in Machine Learning is "classification". This is a learning method for classifying and predicting information by category, such as "judging red apples by looking at images" and "separating purchases and non-purchases on e-commerce sites".

Regression (supervised learning)

Similar to the above, it is a type of supervised learning and is an effective algorithm when dealing with quantities such as sales information and business growth rate. For example, it can help you predict information such as "Who is the most likely customer to buy from past customer information?"

Clustering (unsupervised learning)

This "clustering" is an extension of "classification". This algorithm divides a collection of similar data by function or category. It is a typical algorithm in unsupervised learning and is useful for predicting future information from past information.

Dimensionality Reduction (unsupervised learning)

In Machine learning, the analysis accuracy may deteriorate if there are too many information features. Dimensionality reduction is an algorithm that promotes compression of information amount and correct information visualisation by reducing the dimension of information (number of feature amounts).

Anomaly Detection

Anomaly detection is the detection and estimation of machine and system failures and failures using information analysis. There are cases where a predetermined threshold value detects anomalies and cases where anomalies are detected even if no threshold value is set.

There are many other Machine Learning algorithms. You can refer to Microsoft's cheat sheet etc., for which algorithm to incorporate in Machine Learning.

Types of Machine Learning

Machine Learning methods are a set of tasks aimed at testing hypotheses and finding optimal solutions using Artificial Intelligence. There are three directions:

Supervised Learning

In supervised learning, the data to be analysed are classified beforehand in order to tell the ML system which patterns to search for. The automatic classification of images is learned according to this principle: First, images are manually marked concerning certain variables (e.g. whether it is a sad, happy or neutral facial expression); After creating examples thousands of times, an algorithm can then automatically categorise the image data.

For example, we have data on the income of an online store for six months of operation. We know how many products were sold, how much money was spent on customer acquisition, ROI, average check, number of clicks, bounces and other metrics. The machine's task is to analyse the entire array of data and issue an income forecast for the upcoming period - month, quarter, six months or a year. It is a regressive problem-solving method.

Another example. Based on the array of data and selection criteria, it is necessary to determine whether the text of the letter to the e-mail is spam. Or, having data on the academic performance of schoolchildren in subjects, knowing their IQs on tests, gender and age, you need to help graduates decide on career guidance. The analytical engine seeks out and checks standard features and compares and classifies test results, grades in the school curriculum, and a mindset. It makes a forecast based on the data. These are classification tasks.

Unsupervised Learning

With unsupervised learning, the data to be analysed do not have any previously classified names. Therefore, the algorithm must not be provided with exact target specifications in the preceding training phase. Instead, the ML system itself looks for whatever patterns it can find. Unsupervised learning methods are, therefore, preferred for exploring large data sets. Unsupervised technologies are currently relatively uncommon in practice (except for cybersecurity).

For example, let's say we know the weight, height and body type data of 10,000 potential buyers of jumpers of a particular style. We load the information into the machine to divide clients into clusters according to the available data. As a result, we will get several categories of people with similar characteristics to release a jumper of the desired style for them. These are clustering tasks. Another example. To describe any phenomenon, you have to use 200-300 characteristics. Accordingly, it is complicated to visualise such data, and it is simply impossible to understand them. The analytical system is tasked with processing an array of characteristics and choosing similar ones, compressing data to 2-5-10 characteristics. These are dimensionality reduction problems.

Reinforcement Learning

The method in which an algorithm learns through reward and punishment is described as reinforcement learning. A reinforcement algorithm learns through pure trial and error whether a goal will be achieved (reward) or not (discipline). Reinforcement learning is used, for example, when training chess programs: In a (simulated) game against other chess programs, a system can learn very quickly whether a specific behaviour led to the desired goal, namely victory (reward) or not (punishment). Reinforcement learning is also the training foundation of Google's AlphaGo, the program that defeated the best human players in Go's complex game.

Advantages and Disadvantages

The procedures in supervised learning are easy to understand due to their structure. It is possible to compare different processes, parameterise them, and find an optimal solution for the application. The interpretation of the data is easier than with unsupervised learning methods due to the given traceability.

However, the disadvantage is that the manual work involved in preparing the data is often very high.

The advantages of unsupervised learning consist of fully automated parts. These can produce a perfect forecast of new data or even create new content. The model learns with each new data set and, at the same time, refines its calculations and classifications. Manual intervention is no longer necessary. Neural networks and the classic understanding of Artificial Intelligence are based on this self-learning process.

By teaching these models, they are more and more adapted to input data. From a specific point in time, this leads to what is known as overfitting, in which the model has good forecasts concerning a known data category. However, new, unknown data are no longer correctly assigned. In addition, underfitting can occur, in which too little data has been provided for the model structure, and the classification is, therefore, too imprecise. This also leads to poor forecast results.

When a sufficiently trained model, i.e. neither overfitted nor under fitted, can only be found out through trial and error. This is a very laborious process.

Requirements for ML

To survive, machine learning must have all of the following factors:

Data - usually found in some form as part of the product. They need to be adapted to the needs of Machine Learning. Data collection and screening, and feature selection are critical steps.

Model - usually done in advance and takes a long time.

Forecasting -   Using a model to classify/describe new information. Many times, causes a choice in a specific course of action (e.g. marking a deal as a potential fraud).

In most sites/products, Machine Learning will improve metrics important to the business - interaction with users, sales, customer feedback and the like. We live in a world that produces and needs more information than at any other time in history.

A significant portion of the population uses the Internet and smartphone to perform daily operations such as checking a bank account, ordering products from the supermarket and buying tickets to a movie or show. In any such action, the owners of the site or app can accumulate a lot of data - on which pages on the site the customer visited and what he chose to buy, the amount of time a customer spends on each page before moving on to the next page and many other behavioural characteristics.

Today's challenge is not collecting or storing the data but analysing and producing insights that will enable us to give our customers a better service. In fact, it is a transformation of raw data into information, that is, a database that can be searched and specific questions asked. The more we understand what characterises a particular customer, the more we will be able to provide him with quality and tailored consumer experience that will make him come back to us in the future and differentiate us from the competition.

Suppose a women's clothing company wants to develop a forecasting model in order to provide better fashion recommendations to its customers. This can certainly be done with the help of computational learning.

Based on sales data and customer surveys only, it is possible to recommend to women you do not know about fashion items that you have never seen in a field that you have no idea about.

Machine learning in data science

In data science, machine learning is used in a variety of ways, including:

Predictive modelling: Machine learning algorithms can be used to build models that can predict the likelihood of a certain event or the value of a target variable based on a set of input features. For example, a machine learning model might be used to predict the likelihood that a customer will churn based on their past behaviour.

Classification: Machine learning algorithms can be used to classify data into different categories or classes. For example, a machine learning algorithm might be used to classify emails as spam or not spam or to classify images as containing a certain object or not.

Clustering: Machine learning algorithms can be used to group data points into clusters based on similarities or shared characteristics. This can be useful for tasks such as customer segmentation or data exploration.

Anomaly detection: Machine learning algorithms can be used to identify unusual or unexpected patterns in data, which can indicate anomalies or potential problems.

Deep Learning of Neural Networks

The development of technology has lifted humanity to unprecedented heights. Areas of medicine, safety, training and other types of care have peaked. But that's not all. Artificial intelligence is the next important thing in the world of technology and computer science, but to understand it, it is important to know what it consists of. It is important to know what deep learning and an artificial neural network are.

The field of AI technologies is highly developed and interesting. These two tools, which are used in artificial intelligence, effectively solve complex problems and develop even higher science standards.

It is safe to say that such a mechanism is a transition to a new level of technology. Today's companies have already realised its importance and have started using it in most cases. Take Google, for example. Google uses the AI search engine to learn from its users. If you're looking for something in its search bar, like a "portable computer," and after you get the results, you've just taught Google's AI that "portable computer" is what you click on. I wonder how it works? Let's dive deeper and find out.

Understanding Deep learning

Deep learning is a subfield of machine learning based on artificial neural networks, which are complex systems inspired by the human brain's structure and function. Deep learning algorithms are able to learn from data and improve their performance over time, and they have been successful in a wide range of applications, including image and speech recognition, natural language processing, and predictive modelling.

In data science, deep learning is used to analyse large datasets and build predictive models. It is particularly well suited for tasks that involve analysing unstructured data, such as images, audio, and text.

For example, deep learning algorithms can build image recognition systems that can identify objects, scenes, and people in images. They can also be used to build natural language processing systems that can understand and respond to human language or build predictive models that can make accurate forecasts based on historical data.

Technological advances such as driverless cars need thousands of videos and images to recognise every situation to be safe. To do these things, a computer using deep learning techniques asks for a large amount of training data (this is the work of neural networks; we'll return to that a little later). Recent improvements in deep learning have been brought to the point where it outperforms people in certain tasks.

How it works

As mentioned above, deep learning uses neural networks to perform such tasks. In most cases, deep-learning AI is called a deep neural network. The word deep in this term refers to hidden layers in a neural network.

Deep learning models are trained by obtaining enough data and data architectures from neural networks that study functions directly from data without manual labour. Neural Networks (NN) are as connected as our biological neural networks. Such systems are designed to adapt to situational needs. Once neural networks identify results for a particular object, the next time, NN systems can determine whether it is the same object or not. Neural networks don't recognize objects the way we do; they realise objects because of their unique functions.

Artificial neural networks

One of the most common and popular deep learning types is conventional neural networks, abbreviated to CNN. It combines the studied functions with input and uses 2D drill layers, making it a good fit for 2D data processing. For example, it could be images or sheets of the coordinate plane.

Conventional neural networks work so that there is no longer any need to remove signs manually. It extracts traits directly from the images. Artificial neural networks have automatic traits. This makes deep learning models ideal for computer vision tasks such as object classification.

CNN learns to detect different features using the number of hidden layers. Each number of the hidden layer increases the complexity of the functions of the image studied. CNN explores different features at each level.

Common examples

According to sources, there are three most commonly used ways to use deep learning to classify objects:

Transfer training: The learning approach is mainly used in deep learning applications. This is achieved by having an existing network and adding new data to previously unknown classes. This allows you to classify only certain objects. Rather than view all the different objects until the right one is found. So, it's much better to save time because instead of reducing the amount of image processing.

Learning from scratch: It is mainly used for new applications with many weekend categories. It starts by collecting many tagged datasets and designing a network architecture to explore functions. This method takes a little longer, from days to weeks of training. However, transfer training can take hours or minutes.

Extracting the signs: Not as popular as the methods mentioned earlier, but still widely used. This method is used for a more specialized approach to deep learning. It uses the network as a means of retrieving functions. Because the layers in conventional neural networks are designed to study certain functions from images, you can remove these features and make their inputs for the machine learning model.

what other types of neural networks?

Although a conventional neural network can be considered a standard neural network expanded in space using common weights, there are also several different types.

This artificial neural network recognises sequences such as speech or text. The recurrent neural network, rather than the usual one, expands over time due to ribs, which move on to the next time step. Not the next layer on the same time step.

And there's also a Recursive Neural Network (RNN). This RNN system does not have a time aspect for the input sequence, but input must be handled hierarchically.

Neural networks in action

Artificial neural networks are prevalent among stock market experts. NN systems can use "algorithmic trading." It can apply to financial markets, stocks, interest rates, and currencies. Neural network algorithms can find undervalued stocks, improve existing stock models, and use deep learning. To find ways to optimise the algorithm as the market changes. Understanding the real benefits of neural networks in real-life situations can be challenging.

Because neural networks are very flexible, they can be used to recognise different complex images and predict problems. Alternatively, the NN system can predict business, detect cancer by image and identify faces in social media images.

Deep learning in action

Real examples are not only in neural networks. Deep learning can also be described as some of the following creations:

- Virtual assistants.
- Chatbots or service bots.
- Individual shopping and entertainment.
- Imagine colouring (using algorithms to recreate true colours on black and white images).

What are the differences between DL and NN?

With all this information, it becomes clear that deep learning and neural networks are strongly connected and probably won't work well if they are separated. To understand what deep learning is and what neural networks are, it is crucial to know the basic conclusion.

Neural networks transmit data in the form of input and output values. It is used to transmit data via connections. While deep learning is associated with the transformation and extraction of function. Which is trying to establish a link between the stimulus and the corresponding neural reactions present in the brain. In other words, neural networks are used to manage natural resources, process management, transport management, and decision-making. While deep learning is used for automatic speech recognition, image recognition, etc.

To sum up, we can say that deep learning and neural network complement each other. And they will also develop into an even greater technological miracle than they do today. Artificial intelligence is the next step in our era, and the more experience it has, the more benefits it will bring to society.

Databases

Data Science refers to learning from and analysing large amounts of information. One of the core competencies of data scientists is managing relational databases. First, we must get the data out of the database so we can explore it. In this context, SQL becomes useful. While many cutting-edge businesses have adapted NoSQL for product management, SQL is still often the best option for customer relationship management systems, business intelligence platforms, and back-office procedures.

Database definitions

A database is a collection of organised data that is stored and accessed electronically. In data science, databases are used to store and manage large amounts of data, and they play a key role in many data-driven applications and analyses.

Database types

There are several types of databases that are commonly used in data science, including:

Relational databases: Relational databases are organised into tables, with rows representing data records and columns representing data fields. They are used to store structured data and are well-suited for tasks such as data storage and retrieval.

Non-relational databases: Non-relational databases, also known as NoSQL databases, are used to store unstructured data or data with a complex structure. They are designed to scale horizontally and are often used to store large amounts of data.

Time-series databases: Time-series databases are specialized databases designed to store and analyse time-stamped data, such as sensor readings or financial data. They are optimised for tasks such as querying and aggregating data over time.

Graph databases: Graph databases are used to store and analyse data that is organised as a network of interconnected nodes and edges. They are well suited for tasks such as modelling complex relationships and analysing social networks.

Object-oriented databases: Object-oriented databases are used to store and manipulate objects, which are data structures that combine data and behaviours. They are used to store complex data structures and are often used in object-oriented programming languages. Examples of object-oriented databases include MongoDB and Apache Cassandra.

Relational database

As mentioned above, a relational database is a type of database that is organised into tables, with rows representing data records and columns representing data fields. It is designed to store structured data and is well-suited for data storage and retrieval tasks.

Relational databases use structured query language (SQL) to store, retrieve, and manipulate data. SQL is a programming language designed to manage data held in a relational database management system (RDBMS).

In a relational database, data is organised into tables, also known as relations. Each table has a specific structure, with a set of columns that define the data fields and a set of rows that represent the data records. Tables can be related to one another by using keys, which are fields that uniquely identify a record in a table.

For example, consider a database that stores information about customers and orders. The database might have two tables: one for customer data and one for order data. The customer table might have columns for customer ID, name, and address, and the order table might have columns for order ID, customer ID, and product ID. The customer ID column in the order table would be a foreign key, linking the order table to the customer table.

Relational databases are widely used in many applications, including business, finance, and healthcare. They are known for their reliability, scalability, and ability to support complex queries and transactions. Examples of relational databases include MySQL, Oracle, and Microsoft SQL Server.

Non-relational database

Non-relational databases, also known as NoSQL databases, are used to store unstructured data or data with a complex structure. They are designed to scale horizontally and are often used to store large amounts of data.

Unlike relational databases, which use structured query language (SQL) to store and manipulate data, non-relational databases use different data models and query languages. They are often designed to support specific data storage and access patterns, such as quickly storing and retrieving large amounts of data or supporting real-time access to data.

There are several different types of non-relational databases, including:

- *Document databases:* Document databases store data as documents, which are self-contained data units that can be accessed and manipulated independently. Examples of document databases include MongoDB and Couchbase.
- *Column-oriented databases:* Column-oriented databases store data in columns rather than rows. They are designed to support fast queries and data aggregation and are often used in big data and analytics applications. Examples of column-oriented databases include Cassandra and HBase.
- *Key-value stores:* Key-value stores store data as a collection of keys and values, with the keys used to index and retrieve the values. They are designed to support fast data access and are often used in applications that require real-time data access. Examples of key-value stores include Redis and DynamoDB.

- *Graph databases:* Graph databases store data as a network of interconnected nodes and edges. They are used to model and analyse complex relationships and are often used in social network

Time-series databases

Time-series databases are specialised databases designed to store and analyse time-stamped data, such as sensor readings or financial data. They are optimised for tasks such as querying and aggregating data over time and are often used in applications that require real-time data processing and analysis.

In a time-series database, data is organised into time-stamped records, representing a measurement or event at a specific point in time. Time-series databases typically support various data types, including numerical, definite, and binary data.

Time-series databases use specialised query languages and data structures to support fast queries and data aggregation over time. They often include compression, data retention policies, and the ability to handle large volumes of data.

Time-series databases are used in a wide range of applications, including the Internet of Things (IoT), finance, and healthcare. They are known for handling large volumes of data and supporting real-time data processing and analysis. Examples of time-series databases include InfluxDB and Prometheus.

Object-oriented databases

Object-oriented databases store and manipulate objects, which are data structures that combine data and behaviours. They are used to store complex data structures and are often used in object-oriented programming languages.

In an object-oriented database, data is stored as objects rather than as rows and columns in a table. Objects can have attributes (data fields) and methods (behaviours) associated with them, and they can be related to one another through inheritance and other object-oriented concepts.

Object-oriented databases use object-oriented query languages to store, retrieve, and manipulate data. They are often used in applications that require complex data manipulation and analysis, such as scientific simulations and data modelling.

Object-oriented databases are used in a wide range of applications, including scientific research, data modelling, and business applications. They are known for supporting complex data structures and data manipulation. Examples of object-oriented databases include MongoDB and Apache Cassandra.

Programming

Data scientists use programming to process, analyse, and visualise data and build and deploy machine learning models and other data-driven applications. Programming is a critical aspect of data science. It involves using a programming language to write code that can perform a specific task or solve a problem.

Many programming languages are commonly used in data science, including:

Python: Python is a popular programming language that is widely used in data science. It has a large and active community of users and a wide range of libraries and tools for data processing, analysis, and visualisation.

R: R is a programming language specifically designed for statistical computing and data analysis. It has many libraries and tools for statistical analysis and visualisation and is widely used in academia and the data science industry.

SQL: SQL (Structured Query Language) is a programming language designed to manage data held in a relational database management system (RDBMS). Data scientists use SQL to extract, manipulate, and analyse data stored in a database.

Java: Java is a popular programming language that is widely used in data science, particularly for building large-scale applications and distributed systems.

C++: C++ is a programming language that is known for its performance and speed. It is often used in data science for tasks that require high-performance computing, such as machine learning and data analysis.

Programming skills required for data science

Several programming skills are important for data science, including:

Data manipulation and cleaning: Data scientists need to be able to extract, transform, and clean data in order to prepare it for analysis. This often requires skills such as filtering, sorting, and aggregating data and handling missing or invalid data.

Data visualisation: Data scientists need to be able to visualise data in order to understand trends, patterns, and relationships. This requires skills in creating charts, plots, and other visualisations using tools such as Python's Matplotlib or R's ggplot2.

Machine learning: Data scientists need to be familiar with machine learning algorithms and techniques and be able to implement and apply them using tools such as Python's scikit-learn or R's caret package.

Statistical analysis: Data scientists need to be familiar with statistical concepts and techniques and be able to apply them using tools such as Python's NumPy or R's base package.

Database management: Data scientists often need to work with databases, and they need to be familiar with SQL and other database management languages in order to extract, manipulate, and analyse data stored in a database.

Programming language: Python

Python is a popular, general-purpose programming language that is widely used in data science and other fields. It is known for its simplicity, readability, and flexibility, as well as its large and active community of users.

Some key features of Python include:

High-level language: Python is a high-level language. It is easier to read and write and more abstract from the underlying hardware than low-level languages such as C or Assembly.

Dynamic typing: Python uses dynamic typing, meaning that variables do not have fixed data types, and the variable type is determined at runtime. This makes Python very flexible, but it can also make it slower than statically-typed languages such as C or Java.

Object-oriented programming: Python supports object-oriented programming, which is a programming paradigm based on the concept of "objects", which are data structures that combine data and behaviours.

Large ecosystem: Python has a large and active community of users, and it has a wide range of libraries and tools for tasks such as data processing, analysis, visualisation, and machine learning.

Use of Python in data science

Here are a few examples of how Python is used in data science:

Data manipulation and cleaning: Python has several libraries and tools for extracting, transforming, and cleaning data, such as NumPy, pandas, and scikit-learn. Data scientists use these tools to prepare data for analysis and modelling.

Data visualisation: Python has a number of libraries and tools for creating charts, plots, and other visualisations, such as Matplotlib and Seaborn. Data scientists use these tools to understand trends, patterns, and relationships in data.

Machine learning: Python has a number of libraries and tools for machine learning, such as scikit-learn and TensorFlow. Data scientists use these tools to build and deploy machine learning models, which are algorithms that can learn from data and improve their performance over time.

Statistical analysis: Python has a number of libraries and tools for statistical analysis, such as NumPy and scipy. Data scientists use these tools to perform statistical tests, calculate summary statistics, and fit statistical models.

Data analysis with Python

Here is a simple example of using Python for *data analysis*:

Suppose we have a dataset containing information about a company's sales in a particular year. This dataset is stored in a CSV (Comma Separated Values) file, which can be read into a Python program using the csv module.

```
import csv

# Open the CSV file and read the data into a list of dictionaries
with open('sales.csv', 'r') as f:
    reader = csv.DictReader(f)
    data = list(reader)

# Print the total number of rows in the dataset
print(len(data))

# Calculate the total sales for the year
total_sales = 0
for row in data:
    total_sales += float(row['sales'])
print(total_sales)

# Calculate the average sales per month
average_sales = total_sales / 12
print(average_sales)
```

This code reads the data from the CSV file into a list of dictionaries, where each dictionary represents a row in the file, and the keys are the column names. It then calculates the total sales for the year by looping through the rows and adding up the values in the **'sales'** column. Finally, it calculates the average monthly sales by dividing the total sales by the number of months.

Here is a simple example of using Python for ***data cleaning***:

```
import csv
```

```
# Open the CSV file and read the data into a list of diction-
aries
with open('sales.csv', 'r') as f:
    reader = csv.DictReader(f)
    data = list(reader)

# Remove rows with missing or invalid values
cleaned_data = []
for row in data:
    if row['sales'] and row['region'] and row['month'] in
['Jan', 'Feb', 'Mar', 'Apr', 'May', 'Jun', 'Jul', 'Aug', 'Sep', 'Oct',
'Nov', 'Dec']:
        cleaned_data.append(row)

# Write the cleaned data to a new CSV file
with open('cleaned_sales.csv', 'w') as f:
    fieldnames = ['month', 'region', 'sales']
    writer = csv.DictWriter(f, fieldnames=fieldnames)
    writer.writeheader()
    for row in cleaned_data:
        writer.writerow(row)
```

This code reads the data from the CSV file into a list of dictionaries and then iterates through the rows. For each row, it
checks whether the values for the **'sales'**, **'region'**, and **'month'**
columns are present and valid. If all of these values are present
and valid, the row is added to a new list called **cleaned_data**.
Otherwise, the row is skipped.

Finally, the code writes the cleaned data to a new CSV file,
with only the **'month'**, **'region'**, and **'sales'** columns included.

This is just a very basic example of data cleaning with Python. In a real-world dataset, there may be many more columns
and many more types of invalid or missing data that need to be

identified and handled. There are also many specialized libraries and tools available for data cleaning in Python, such as **pandas**, numpy, and **scipy**.

Python modules for Data Science
Pandas

Pandas is a library written for the Python programming language for data manipulation and analysis. In particular, it offers data structures and operations for manipulating numerical tables and time series. Pandas is free software released under the three-clause BSD license.

Website: http://pandas.pydata.org/

Statsmodels

Statsmodels is a Python module that allows users to explore data, estimate statistical models, and perform statistical tests. An extensive list of descriptive statistics, statistical tests, plotting functions, and result statistics is available for different data types and each estimator.

Website: http://statsmodels.sourceforge.net/

scikit-learn

scikit-learn is an open-source library for Python. It features various classification, regression and clustering algorithms, including support vector machines, logistic regression, naive Bayes, random forests, gradient boosting, k-means and DBSCAN. It is designed to interoperate with the Python numerical and scientific libraries NumPy and SciPy.

Website: http://scikit-learn.org/stable/

Mlpy

Mlpy is a Python machine-learning library built on top of NumPy/SciPy, the GNU Scientific Library. mlpy provides a wide range of machine-learning methods for a supervised and unsupervised problem.mlpy is multi-platform, it works with Python 2 and 3.

Website: http://mlpy.sourceforge.net/

NumPy

NumPy is an open-source extension module for Python. The module NumPy provides fast precompiled functions for numerical routines.

It adds support to Python for large, multi-dimensional arrays and matrices. Besides that, it supplies a large library of high-level mathematical functions to operate on these arrays

Website: http://www.numpy.org/

SciPy

SciPy is widely used in scientific and technical computing. SciPy contains modules for optimisation, linear algebra, integration, interpolation, special functions, FFT, signal and image processing, ODE solvers, and other common science and engineering tasks.

Website: http://www.scipy.org/

matplotlib

matplotlib is a plotting library for NumPy.
Website: http://matplotlib.org/

NLTK

The Natural Language Toolkit, or more commonly NLTK, is a suite of libraries and programs for statistical natural language processing (NLP) for Python. NLTK includes graphical demonstrations and sample data. NLTK has been used successfully as a platform for prototyping and building research systems
Website: http://www.nltk.org/

Theano

Theano is a Python library that allows you to define, optimise, and evaluate mathematical expressions involving multi-dimensional arrays efficiently
Website: http://deeplearning.net/software/theano/

nolearn

This package contains several utility modules that are helpful with machine learning tasks. Most of the modules work together with scikit-learn; others are more generally useful.
https://pythonhosted.org/nolearn/

PyBrain

PyBrain is short for Python-Based Reinforcement Learning, Artificial Intelligence and Neural Network Library. Its goal is to offer flexible, easy-to-use yet still powerful algorithms for Machine Learning Tasks and various predefined environments to test and compare your algorithms.
http://pybrain.org/

Orange

Orange is a component-based data mining and machine learning software suite. It features a visual programming front-end for explorative data analysis and visualisation and Python bindings and libraries for scripting. It includes a set of components for data pre-processing, feature scoring and filtering, modelling, model evaluation, and exploration techniques. It is implemented in C++ and Python. Its graphical user interface builds upon the cross-platform Qt framework.

Unlike its competitors scikit-learn and mlpy, Orange does not tie into NumPy and its ecosystem of tools; it focuses on traditional, symbolic algorithms more than numeric ones.

http://orange.biolab.si/

Keras

Keras is a minimalist, highly modular neural network library in the spirit of Torch, written in Python that uses Theano under the hood for fast tensor manipulation on GPU and CPU. It was developed with a focus on enabling fast experimentation.

http://keras.io/

Hebel

Hebel is a library for deep learning with neural networks in Python using GPU acceleration with CUDA through PyCUDA. It implements the most important types of neural network models and offers a variety of different activation functions and training methods, such as momentum, Nesterov momentum, dropout, and early stopping.

https://github.com/hannes-brt/hebel

Python codes for data science

Here are a few examples of Python code that could be used for data science tasks:

Importing and cleaning data:

```
import pandas as pd

# Read a CSV file into a Pandas DataFrame
df = pd.read_csv("data.csv")

# Remove rows with missing values
df.dropna(inplace=True)

# Replace missing values with the mean value of the column
df.fillna(df.mean(), inplace=True)

# Normalize the data by scaling it to have a mean of 0 and a
standard deviation of 1
df = (df - df.mean()) / df.std()
```

Exploratory data analysis:

```
import matplotlib.pyplot as plt

# Plot a histogram of a column
plt.hist(df["column_name"], bins=20)
plt.xlabel("Column name")
plt.ylabel("Frequency")
plt.title("Histogram of column values")
plt.show()

# Plot a scatterplot of two columns
plt.scatter(df["column_1"], df["column_2"])
plt.xlabel("Column 1")
plt.ylabel("Column 2")
plt.title("Scatterplot of columns")
plt.show()
```

Building a machine learning model:

import sklearn

 # Split the data into a training set and a test set
X_train, X_test, y_train, y_test = sklearn.model_selection.train_test_split(X, y, test_size=0.2)

 # Train a linear regression model

Programming language: R

R is a programming language and software environment for statistical computing and graphics. Statisticians, data scientists, and data analysts widely use it for tasks such as data manipulation, visualisation, and statistical modelling.

Some of the key features of R include:

- A large collection of built-in functions and libraries for tasks such as statistical analysis, machine learning, data manipulation, and visualisation.
- A flexible and expressive syntax allows you to write code that is easy to read and understand.
- An interactive interpreter allows you to try out small pieces of code and see their results immediately.
- A strong community of users and developers has contributed a wide range of packages and tools for tasks such as data import, data manipulation, and machine learning.

R created for data science

The R programming language, unlike Python, was explicitly created to support mathematical computing and data analysis.

R is widely used by data scientists worldwide and with good reason. All of the features required by data scientists are available in R. According to a 2014 survey by O'Reilly Media, R is the most popular programming language used by data analysts.

The R programming language allows you to do data science calculations without a compiler, making code development more efficient. In addition, R is a statistical language, so statistical models can easily be converted into code with R.

Example of using R for data analysis

```
# Load the data from a CSV file
sales <- read.csv('sales.csv')

# Calculate the total sales for the year
total_sales <- sum(sales$sales)
print(total_sales)

# Calculate the average sales per month
average_sales <- total_sales / 12
print(average_sales)

# Create a bar plot of the sales data
barplot(sales$sales,    xlab='Month',    ylab='Sales',
main='Monthly Sales')
```

This code reads the data from the CSV file into a data frame, which is a table of data with rows and columns. It then calculates the total sales for the year by summing the values in the **'sales'** column and calculates the average sales per month by dividing the total sales by the number of months. Finally, it creates a bar plot of the sales data, with the months on the x-axis and the sales on the y-axis.

R is particularly well-suited for data visualisation and statistical analysis and is often used in finance, marketing, and biology fields. Many resources are available for learning R, including online tutorials, books, and video courses.

Free R learning resources

Take a look at these freely available books (but buy some of them to support the authors' work):

R for Data Science
https://r4ds.had.co.nz/
R Programming for Data Science
https://bookdown.org/rdpeng/rprogdatascience/
Hands-On Programming with R
https://rstudio-education.github.io/hopr/
Efficient R programming
https://csgillespie.github.io/efficientR/
Welcome | Advanced R
https://adv-r.hadley.nz/
Advanced R Solutions
https://advanced-r-solutions.rbind.io/
R Cookbook, 2nd Edition
https://rc2e.com/
Welcome! | R Packages
https://r-pkgs.org/
Welcome | ggplot2
https://ggplot2-book.org/
R Graphics Cookbook, 2nd edition
https://r-graphics.org/
Fundamentals of Data Visualisation
https://clauswilke.com/dataviz/
Interactive web-based data visualisation with R, Plotly, and shiny
https://plotly-r.com/
Engineering Production-Grade Shiny Apps
https://plotly-r.com/
JavaScript 4 Shiny - Field Notes
https://connect.thinkr.fr/js4shinyfieldnotes/
Statistical Inference via Data Science

https://moderndive.com/
Hands-On Machine Learning with R
https://bradleyboehmke.github.io/HOML/
index.utf8.md
https://koalaverse.github.io/homlr/
Welcome to Text Mining with R
https://www.tidytextmining.com/
The tidyverse style guide
https://style.tidyverse.org/
R Markdown: The Definitive Guide
https://bookdown.org/yihui/rmarkdown/
R Markdown Cookbook
https://bookdown.org/yihui/rmarkdown-cookbook/
Bookdown: Authoring Books and Technical Documents with R Markdown
https://bookdown.org/yihui/bookdown/
Blogdown: Creating Websites with R Markdown
https://bookdown.org/yihui/blogdown/

R – codes for data analysis

Here are a few examples of R code that could be used for data science tasks:

Importing and cleaning data:

```
# Read a CSV file into a data frame
df <- read.csv("data.csv")

# Remove rows with missing values
df <- df[complete.cases(df), ]

# Replace missing values with the mean value of the column
df[is.na(df)] <- lapply(df, mean, na.rm=TRUE)
```

 # Normalize the data by scaling it to have a mean of 0 and a standard deviation of 1
df <- scale(df)

Exploratory data analysis:

 # Plot a histogram of a column
hist(df$column_name, breaks=20, xlab="Column name", ylab="Frequency", main="Histogram of column values")

 # Plot a scatterplot of two columns
plot(df$column_1, df$column_2, xlab="Column 1", ylab="Column 2", main="Scatterplot of columns")

Building a machine learning model:

 # Split the data into a training set and a test set
train_indices <- createDataPartition(df$target, p=0.8, list=FALSE)
train <- df[train_indices,]
test <- df[-train_indices,]

 # Train a linear regression model
model <- lm(target ~ ., data=train)

 # Make predictions on the test set
predictions <- predict(model, test)

 # Calculate the mean squared error
mse <- mean((predictions - test$target)^2)

SQL

SQL (Structured Query Language) is a programming language used to manage and manipulate data stored in relational database management systems (RDBMS). It is a standard language for interacting with databases and is widely used in the field of data science.

SQL is important for data science because it allows data scientists to extract and analyse data from databases and other sources. With SQL, data scientists can query, update, and delete data; create and modify tables and schemas, and perform other tasks that are necessary for data analysis.

Here are some examples of SQL databases:

MySQL: An open-source RDBMS that is widely used for web applications and data analysis.

Oracle: A commercial RDBMS developed by Oracle Corporation.

Microsoft SQL Server: A RDBMS developed by Microsoft.

PostgreSQL: An open-source RDBMS is known for its strong support for SQL and ability to handle large amounts of data.

The use of SQL in data science

SQL is often used in data science to retrieve and manipulate data from databases and other sources. Some common tasks that data scientists might perform using SQL in their work include:

Querying data: Data scientists use SQL to retrieve specific data from a database or other sources. For example, they might use SQL to select specific columns from a table or filter rows based on certain criteria.

Cleaning and transforming data: Data scientists often use SQL to clean and transform data to make it more suitable for analysis. For example, they might use SQL to remove duplicates, fix errors, or combine data from multiple tables.

Aggregating and summarising data: SQL can group and summarise data in various ways. For example, data scientists might use SQL to calculate a particular column's average, minimum, or maximum value or to group data by a certain attribute.

Creating and modifying tables: Data scientists may use SQL to create or modify new tables in a database. For example, they might use SQL to add or delete columns or change a column's data type.

SQL is an essential tool for data scientists, as it allows them to efficiently retrieve, manipulate, and analyse data from various sources.

MySQL

MySQL is an open-source relational database management system (RDBMS) that is widely used for web applications and data analysis. It is developed, distributed, and supported by Oracle Corporation.

MySQL is based on the SQL (Structured Query Language) programming language, which manages and manipulates data stored in relational databases. With MySQL, users can create and modify databases, tables, and other database objects; insert, update, and delete data; and perform various other tasks related to database management.

MySQL is known for its reliability, speed, and ease of use. It is also highly flexible, as it can be used on a variety of platforms, including Windows, Linux, and Mac OS. In addition, MySQL supports a wide range of programming languages, including PHP, Java, C++, and Python, making it easy to integrate with other systems and applications.

MySQL is a popular and powerful choice for storing and managing data in various contexts, including web development, data analysis, and business applications.

Non-SQL

Non-SQL, or NoSQL, refers to databases that do not use the Structured Query Language (SQL) to manipulate and manage data. Non-SQL databases are designed to handle large amounts of unstructured, semi-structured, or structured data, and are often used in situations where traditional relational databases are not well-suited.

Some examples of non-SQL databases include:

MongoDB: A popular NoSQL database that stores data in the form of flexible, JSON-like documents.

Cassandra: A NoSQL database designed for high scalability and availability with no single point of failure.

HBase: An open-source, distributed NoSQL database built on top of the Hadoop ecosystem.

Redis: An in-memory data store that can be used as a database, cache, or message broker.

Non-SQL databases provide an alternative to traditional relational databases for storing and managing data in various contexts, including web applications, big data, and real-time analytics. They are also well-suited for handling high volumes of writes and reads and for supporting real-time data processing and analytics. Non-SQL databases are often used when data is too large or complex to be effectively stored and managed in a traditional relational database.

SQL query codes for data analysis

Here is an example of a simple SQL query that could be used for data analysis:

```
SELECT
    customer_name,
    SUM(order_total) AS total_spent
FROM orders
```

WHERE order_date BETWEEN '2022-01-01' AND '2022-12-31'
GROUP BY customer_name
ORDER BY total_spent DESC
LIMIT 10;

This query would select the top 10 customers who have spent the most money in the orders table between the start and end dates specified. It does this by selecting the customer name and the sum of their order totals, grouping the results by customer name and ordering the results by the total spent in descending order. The **LIMIT** clause is used to limit the results to the top 10 customers.

This is just one example of a SQL query that could be used for data analysis. There are many other types of queries that could be used to perform different types of analysis on different types of data.

Data Science project ideas

Idea - 1

Here is a project idea that you can use to practice data science skills:

- Identify a problem or question that you want to address using data. This could be a business problem, a social issue, or any other area of interest.
- Collect and clean the data that you will need to address the problem or question. This may involve retrieving data from a database, web scraping, or other data-gathering methods. You will also need to remove any errors or inconsistencies in the data.
- Explore the data to get a better understanding of its characteristics and relationships. Use visualisations and other techniques to identify patterns and trends.
- Build a machine learning model to address the problem or answer the question. This may involve selecting and tuning the appropriate model, training the model on the data, and evaluating its performance.
- Use the model to make predictions or generate insights. Communicate your findings to others through a report, presentation, or other media.

This project will allow you to practice many key important skills in data science, including data collection and cleaning, exploration, modelling, and communication. You can adjust the scope and complexity of the project based on your interests and skill level.

Idea -2

Here is another idea for a data science project:

Choose a dataset to work with. This could be a public dataset from a repository such as Kaggle or UCI Machine Learning Repository or a dataset you have collected.

- Explore the dataset to get a better understanding of its characteristics and relationships. Use visualisations and other techniques to identify patterns and trends.
- Formulate a hypothesis or research question based on your exploration of the data. This should be a question that you can answer using the data and machine learning techniques.
- Preprocess the data as needed to prepare it for modelling. This may involve cleaning the data, scaling or transforming variables, or creating new features.
- Build and evaluate machine learning models to answer the research question or test the hypothesis. This may involve selecting and tuning the appropriate model, training the model on the data, and evaluating its performance.
- Use the model to make predictions or generate insights. Communicate your findings to others through a report, presentation, or other media.

This project will allow you to practice the entire data science process, from data exploration and preparation to model building and evaluation. You can adjust the scope and complexity of the project based on your interests and skill level.

Idea -3

Here is the third idea for a data science project:

Choose a real-world problem that you are interested in solving using data. This could be a problem faced by a company, a social issue, or any other area of interest.

- Identify the data sources that you will need to address the problem. This may involve accessing public datasets, collecting data from web APIs, or collecting data yourself through surveys or other methods.
- Collect and clean the data as needed. This may involve retrieving data from multiple sources, removing errors or inconsistencies, and suitably formatting the data for analysis.
- Explore the data to get a better understanding of its characteristics and relationships. Use visualisations and other techniques to identify patterns and trends.
- Use machine learning techniques to build a model that can help address the problem or generate insights. This may involve selecting and tuning the appropriate model, training the model on the data, and evaluating its performance.
- Use the model to make predictions or generate insights. Communicate your findings to others through a report, presentation, or other media.

This project will allow you to apply data science techniques to a real-world problem of your choice. You can adjust the scope and complexity of the project based on your interests and skill level.

Idea – 4

Here is an exercise that you can use to practice data analytics skills:

- Choose a dataset to work with. This could be a public dataset from a repository such as Kaggle or UCI Machine Learning Repository or a dataset you have collected.
- Load the dataset into a data analysis tool like Excel, Google Sheets, or a programming language like Python or R.
- Explore the data to get a better understanding of its characteristics and relationships. Use visualisations and other techniques to identify patterns and trends.
- Formulate a research question or hypothesis based on your exploration of the data. This should be a question that you can answer using the data and analysis techniques.
- Use appropriate statistical and analytical techniques to answer the research question or test the hypothesis. This may involve calculating summary statistics, testing hypotheses, or building models.

Communicate your findings to others through a report, presentation, or other media.

This exercise will allow you to practice a wide range of data analytics skills, including data exploration, visualisation, statistical analysis, and communication. You can adjust the scope and complexity of the exercise based on your interests and skill level.

Data Science use cases

Here are some examples of how data science is in different industries in addition to what was mentioned in the first few pages of this book:

Google

Google uses data science in a wide range of applications and projects. Some examples of how Google uses data science include:

Search and advertising: Google uses data science to improve its search results' quality and relevance and optimise its advertising targeting and bidding algorithms.

Maps and location services: Google uses data science to improve the accuracy and functionality of its maps and location services, such as Google Maps and Google Earth.

Natural language processing: Google uses data science to improve the performance of its natural language processing (NLP) systems, which are used in products such as Google Translate and Google Assistant.

Computer vision: Google uses data science to improve the performance of its computer vision systems, which are used in products such as Google Photos and Google Street View.

Healthcare: Google uses data science to develop new healthcare technologies and applications, such as algorithms for analysing medical images and predicting patient outcomes.

Google relies on data science to drive innovation and improve the performance of its products and services. Data science is a key part of Google's operations, and the company employs a large team of data scientists and engineers to work on data-related projects.

Amazon

Amazon uses data science in a wide range of applications and projects. Some examples of how Amazon uses data science include:

Personalisation: Amazon uses data science to personalise the shopping experience for its customers. For example, the company uses customer behaviour and preferences data to recommend products and display targeted advertisements.

Supply chain optimisation: Amazon uses data science to optimise its supply chain and fulfilment operations. For example, the company uses data on customer demand, inventory levels, and shipping costs to determine the most efficient way to fulfil orders.

Fraud detection: Amazon uses data science to detect fraudulent activity, such as fake reviews and account takeovers.

Forecasting: Amazon uses data science to forecast demand for its products and services, which helps the company manage its inventory and production levels.

Predictive maintenance: Amazon uses data science to predict when equipment and machinery will fail, which helps the company prevent disruptions and improve efficiency.

Amazon uses data science to drive innovation and improve the efficiency and effectiveness of its operations. Data science is a key part of Amazon's business, and the company employs a large team of data scientists and engineers to work on data-related projects.

Microsoft

Microsoft uses data science in a wide range of applications and projects. Some examples of how Microsoft uses data science include:

Software development: Microsoft uses data science to improve the performance and reliability of its software products, such as Windows and Office. For example, the company uses data on customer usage patterns to identify and fix bugs and to optimise the user experience.

Advertising: Microsoft uses data science to improve the targeting and effectiveness of its online advertising products, such as Bing Ads.

Cybersecurity: Microsoft uses data science to improve the security of its products and services. For example, the company uses data on cyber threats and attacks to improve its intrusion detection systems.

Healthcare: Microsoft uses data science to develop new healthcare technologies and applications, such as algorithms for analysing medical images and predicting patient outcomes.

Gaming: Microsoft uses data science to optimise its gaming products' performance and user experiences, such as Xbox and Minecraft.

Microsoft uses data science to drive innovation and improve the performance and security of its products and services. Data science is a key part of Microsoft's operations, and the company employs a large team of data scientists and engineers to work on data-related projects.

Meta (Facebook)

Facebook uses data science in a wide range of applications and projects. Some examples of how Facebook uses data science include:

Personalisation: Facebook uses data science to personalize the user experience for its users. For example, the company uses user behaviour and preferences data to recommend content and display targeted advertisements.

Network analysis: Facebook uses data science to analyse the connections and interactions within its social network. This helps the company understand how people use the platform and identify trends and patterns.

Fraud detection: Facebook uses data science to detect fraudulent activity, such as fake accounts and spam.

Content recommendation: Facebook uses data science to recommend content to users based on their interests and behaviour.

Machine learning: Facebook uses data science and machine learning techniques to improve the performance of its products and services, such as by optimising the delivery of news feed content and improving the image and video recognition.

Facebook uses data science to drive innovation and improve the user experience of its products and services. Data science is a key part of Facebook's operations, and the company employs a large team of data scientists and engineers to work on data-related projects.

Apple

Apple uses data science in a wide range of applications and projects. Some examples of how Apple uses data science include:

Personalisation: Apple uses data science to personalise the user experience for its customers. For example, the company uses customer behaviour and preferences data to recommend products and display targeted advertisements.

Machine learning: Apple uses data science and machine learning techniques to improve the performance of its products and services, such as by optimizing the performance of Siri and improving the image and video recognition.

Healthcare: Apple is using data science to develop new healthcare technologies and applications, such as algorithms for analyzing medical images and predicting patient outcomes.

Supply chain optimisation: Apple uses data science to optimise its supply chain and manufacturing operations. For example, the company uses data on customer demand, inventory levels, and production capacity to determine the most efficient way to produce and distribute its products.

Fraud detection: Apple uses data science to detect fraudulent activity, such as fake reviews and account takeovers.

Overall, Apple uses data science to drive innovation and improve the performance and efficiency of its products and services. Data science is a key part of Apple's operations, and the company employs a large team of data scientists and engineers to work on data-related projects.

Emerging technologies and data science

Artificial intelligence (AI) and machine learning: AI and machine learning technologies are becoming increasingly sophisticated and widely used in data science. These technologies enable data scientists to build more accurate and powerful models, and to automate many tasks that were previously done manually. Emerging technologies have the potential to significantly impact data science and the way that data is collected, analysed, and used.

The IoT refers to the network of connected devices that collect and transmit data over the internet. The proliferation of IoT devices generates a vast amount of data that can be used for data science purposes, such as analysing patterns and trends, predicting outcomes, and optimising processes.

Some examples of emerging technologies that are likely to have an impact on data science include:

Quantum computing

Quantum computers are a new type of computer that use quantum mechanics to perform certain tasks much faster than traditional computers. Quantum computers can revolutionise data science by enabling the analysis of much larger and more complex datasets than is currently possible.

Data science can be impacted by quantum computing in several ways:

Data processing: Quantum computers have the potential to perform certain data processing tasks much faster than traditional computers. For example, quantum computers could be used to analyse large datasets much more quickly, which would enable data scientists to generate insights and make decisions more efficiently.

Machine learning: Quantum computers can potentially improve the performance of machine learning algorithms by enabling the analysis of larger and more complex datasets. Quantum machine learning algorithms are an active area of research, and quantum computers will likely be able to perform certain tasks much more efficiently than traditional computers.

Optimisation: Quantum computers can be used to solve optimisation problems more quickly than traditional computers. This could have applications in areas such as logistics, finance, and supply chain management, where data scientists often need to find the optimal solution to a problem.

To summarise, quantum computing has the potential to significantly impact data science by enabling the analysis of larger and more complex datasets, improving the performance of machine learning algorithms, and solving optimisation problems more efficiently.

However, quantum computers are still in the early stages of development, and it is not yet clear how widely they will be adopted or what their full potential will be.

Metaverse

The metaverse is a virtual shared space created by the convergence of virtually enhanced physical reality and physically persistent virtual space, including the sum of all virtual worlds, augmented realities, and the internet. It is not yet clear how the metaverse will be impacted by data science, as the metaverse concept is still in the early stages of development and not yet fully realized. However, data science will likely play a significant role in the development and operation of the metaverse in several ways:

Data collection and analysis: The metaverse is likely to generate a vast amount of data on user behaviour, interactions, and preferences. Data science techniques will be needed to collect, clean, and analyse this data, understand how the metaverse is used, and identify trends and patterns.

Personalisation: Data science could be used to personalise the user experience in the metaverse by using data on user behaviour and preferences to tailor content and experiences to individual users.

Machine learning: Machine learning algorithms could be used to improve the performance and functionality of the metaverse, such as by optimising the delivery of content and improving virtual assistants' accuracy.

Predictive analytics: Data science could be used to predict user behaviour and outcomes in the metaverse, optimising the user experience and identifying potential problems or opportunities.

Overall, it is likely that data science will play a key role in the development and operation of the metaverse by enabling the collection and analysis of data, personalising the user experience, and improving the performance and functionality of the platform.

Blockchain

Blockchain technology is a decentralized, distributed database that enables secure, transparent, and immutable record-keeping. It has the potential to impact data science in several ways:

Data storage and management: Blockchain technology can store and manage data securely, transparently, and immutable way. This could be particularly useful when the data needs to be shared among multiple parties and there is a need to maintain a verifiable data record.

Data security: Blockchain technology can be used to secure data by providing a decentralised and distributed database that is resistant to tampering and unauthorized access. This could be particularly useful when data privacy and security are critical concerns.

Data interoperability: Blockchain technology can be used to enable data interoperability, which refers to the ability of different systems and platforms to exchange and use data. Using blockchain technology, data scientists can create a common data platform that can be accessed and used by multiple parties, enabling greater collaboration and data sharing.

Data provenance: Blockchain technology can be used to track the origin and history of data, which is known as data provenance. This could be useful in situations where it is important to verify the authenticity and accuracy of the data, such as in scientific research or financial transactions.

So basically, blockchain technology has the potential to significantly impact data science by enabling secure, transparent, and interoperable data storage and management and by enabling the tracking of data provenance.

Autonomous cars

Autonomous cars, also known as self-driving cars, are equipped with sensors, cameras, and other technologies that allow them to navigate and drive without human intervention. Data science is likely to play a significant role in the development and operation of autonomous cars in several ways:

Data collection and analysis: Autonomous cars will generate a vast amount of data on their surroundings, including information on traffic, road conditions, and the behaviour of other vehicles and pedestrians. Data science techniques will be needed to collect, clean, and analyse this data to enable the autonomous car to make informed decisions and navigate safely.

Machine learning: Machine learning algorithms will be used to enable autonomous cars to learn from and adapt to their environment by analysing data on their surroundings and adjusting their behaviour accordingly.

Predictive analytics: Data science could be used to predict the behaviour of other vehicles and pedestrians, which could optimise the route and speed of the autonomous car and identify potential hazards.

Safety: Data science could be used to ensure the safety of autonomous cars by analysing data on past accidents and identifying patterns and trends that could be used to prevent future accidents.

Robotics

Robotics is the branch of engineering that deals with the design, construction, operation, and application of robots. Data science is likely to play a significant role in the development and operation of robotics in several ways:

Data collection and analysis: Robotics systems will generate a vast amount of data on their surroundings, including information on their own performance, the environment they are operating in, and the objects and materials they are interacting with. Data science techniques will be needed to collect, clean, and analyse this data to enable the robotics system to make informed decisions and operate effectively.

Machine learning: Machine learning algorithms will be used to enable robotics systems to learn from and adapt to their environment by analysing data on their surroundings and adjusting their behaviour accordingly.

Predictive analytics: Data science could be used to predict the behaviour of other objects and materials, which could optimise the operation of the robotics system and identify potential hazards.

Safety: Data science could be used to ensure the safety of robotics systems, by analysing data on past accidents and identifying patterns and trends that could be used to prevent future accidents.

Data Science Acronyms
You Need to Know

ACID: *Atomicity, Consistency, Isolation and Durability*

ANOVA: *Analysis of Variance*

AOSD : *Aspect: Oriented Software Development*

AQL: *Annotation Query Language*

AUC: *Area Under the Curve (ROC curve)*

AUROC: *Area Under Receiver Operating Characteristic*

BDA: *Big Data Analytics*

CART: *Classification and Regression Trees*

CCA: *Canonical Correlational Analysis*

CEP: *Complex Event Processing*

CNN: *Convolutional Neural Network;*

COTS: *Commodity off:the: shelf*

CQL: *Cassandra Query Language*

CQL: *Contextual/Common Query Language*

CV: *Cross-Validation*

DAD: *Discover, Access, Distill*

DAG: *Directed Acyclic Graph*

DHSL : *Distributed Hadoop Storage Layer*

FUSE: *Filesystem in Userspace*

GBM: *Gradient Boosting Machine*

GEOFF: *Graph Serialization Format*

GLM: *Generalized Linear Model*

GRU: *Gated Recurrent Unit*

HAR: *Hadoop Archive*

HMM: *Hidden Markov Model*

HPCC: *High-Performance Computing Cluster*

HPIL: *Hadoop Physical Infrastructure Layer*

ICA: *Independent Component Analysis*

IDA: *Initial Data Analysis*

JAQL: *JSON Query Language*

JSON: *JavaScriptObjectNotation Query Language*

KFS: *Kosmos File System*

kNN: *k: Nearest Neighbors*

LB: *LeaderBoard*

LDA: *Latent Dirichlet Allocation or Linear Discriminant Analysis*

LKOV: *Leave:k:Outcross:validation*

LLE: *Locally Linear Embedding*

LOOCV: *Leave:One:Outcross: validation*

DNN: *Deep Neural Network or Deconvolutional Neural Network*

ECL: *Enterprise Control Language*

EDA: *Exploratory Data Analysis, Event-Driven Architecture*

EDA: *Exploratory Data Analysis*

EPN: *Event Processing Nodes*

MDS: *Multidimensional Scaling*

MSE: *Mean Squared Error*

NLDR: *Non: Linear Dimensionality Reduction*

NLP : *Natural Language Processing*

NMF: *Non: Negative Matrix Factorization*

OLAP: *Online Analytical Processing*

OLTP: *Online Transactional Processing*

OOF: *Out Of Fold*

PCA: *Principal Component Analysis*

pLDA: *Probabilistic Latent Semantic Allocation*

PMML: *Predictive Model Markup Language*

R2 : *R: squared (regression metrics)*

RDD: *Resilient Distributed Database*

RF: *Random Forest*

RFE: *Recursive Feature Elimination*

LpO CV: *Leave:p:outcross: validation*

LSA/LSI: *Latent Semantic Allocation/Indexing*

LSTM: *Long Short Term Memory*

LZO: *Lempel–Ziv–Oberhumer*

MAPE: *Mean Absolute Percentage Error*

MCMC: *Markov chain Monte Carlo*

MDM: *Master Data Management*

VC: *Vapnik Chervonekis Dimension*

W3C: *World Wide Web Consortium*

XML: *Extensible Markup Language*

YARN: *Yet Another Resource Manager*

ZFS: *Zettabyte File System by Sun Microsystem*

RMS: *Root Mean Squared Logarithmic Error*
RNN: *Recurrent Neural Network*
ROC : *Receiver Operating Characteristic*
S4 : *Simple Scalable Streaming System*
SMOTE: *Synthetic Minority Oversampling Technique*
SOA: *Service-Oriented Architecture*
SVM: *Support Vector Machine*
TDA: *Topological Data Analysis*
tf:idf: *term frequency, inverse document frequency*
t:SNE: *t: Distributed Stochastic Neighbor Embedding*
UDTF: *User-Defined Tablegenerating Function*
UIMA: *Unstructured Information Management Architecture*

Table of Figures

About the author

Enamul Haque is an author, researcher and managing con-

sultant best known for working with global companies such as Microsoft, Capgemini, Nokia, and HCL Technologies, and the United Nations High Commissioner for Refugees (UNHCR) and International Telecommunication Union (ITU). He works with many Fortune 500 companies on digital transformation, Cloud Adoption, AI-Driven RPA (Intelligent Process Automation) and Service Integration and Management. He writes on IT Service Management, Cloud Computing, AI, IoT and Big Data analytics. He has 26+ years of rich experience in IT transformation.

Enamul shares his industry knowledge among MBA students as a guest lecturer at the University of Coventry, London campus. He also worked very extensively as contributing writer for various newspapers, magazines and other publications. Enamul is multilingual (writes in French, English and Bengali) and lived and worked in many countries, including the USA, Switzerland, Finland, UAE, UK, India and Germany.

Enamul Haque's books include The Ultimate Modern Guide to Cloud Computing, Cloud Service Management and Governance, The Ultimate Modern Guide to Artificial Intelligence, The Ultimate Modern Guide to The Internet of Things, and A Beginner's Guide to Data Science. All his books are written based on real-life experience and as a practitioner of leading-edge industry revolution.

Enamul Haque studied mathematics and analytics (Cours de mathématiques spéciales) at the Swiss Federal Institute of Technology (EPFL), Lausanne and architecture and technology of computer science (license en science Informatique) at the

University of Geneva. He also has a diploma in Artificial Intelligence and Machine Learning from the University of Helsinki.

Enamul Haque has received many accolades and great recognition for his achievements in the IT industry. Nokia Academy has awarded him a Business Leadership Diploma after a year of a successful business development project. He is currently working on a leadership program powered by Harvard. Enamul is an avid enthusiast for sharing his industry knowledge.

Other Books by the Author

The Ultimate Modern Guide to Cloud Computing

The Ultimate Modern Guide to Artificial Intelligence

The Ultimate Modern Guide to the Internet of Things

The Ultimate Modern Guide to Digital Transformation

Enterprise Service Management (ESM)

Cloud Service Management and Governance

Official Website: enamulhaque.co.uk

Notes and References

[1] **Data Camp** - Data Science Salary Expectations in 2022 – Link: https://www.datacamp.com/blog/data-science-salaries

[2] **Usama M. Fayyad** is an American data scientist and co-founder of KDD conferences and ACM SIGKDD association for Knowledge Discovery and Data Mining. He is a speaker on Business Analytics, Data Mining, Data Science, and Big Data. He recently left his role as the Chief Data Officer at Barclays Bank.

[3] **Gregory I. Piatetsky-Shapiro** is a data scientist and the co-founder of the KDD conferences, and co-founder and past chair of the Association for Computing Machinery SIGKDD group for Knowledge Discovery, Data Mining and Data Science.

[4] **Padhraic Smyth** is a Professor of Computer Science in UC Irvine's Donald Bren School of Information and Computer Sciences. He also serves as Director of UC Irvine's Data Science Initiative, and Associate Director for UC Irvine's Center for Machine Learning and Intelligent Systems.

[5] **Drew Conway** is an American data scientist known for his venn diagram definition of data science as well as applying data science to study terrorism. He is currently the founder and CEO at technology startup Alluvium, as well as advisor at multiple technology startups.

[6] **Dhanurjay "DJ" Patil** is an American mathematician and computer scientist who served as the Chief Data Scientist of the United States Office of Science and Technology Policy. from 2015 to 2017. He is the Head of Technology for Devoted Health.

[7] **NVP** - Big Data and AI Executive Survey 2021. Link: https://c6abb8db-514c-4f5b-b5a1-

fc710f1e464e.filesusr.com/ugd/e5361a_d59b4629443945a0b06
61d494abb5233.pdf

[8] FAIR Principles - https://www.go-fair.org/fair-principles/

[9] Operations Research Analysts – Link:
https://www.bls.gov/ooh/math/operations-research-analysts.htm

[10] **Saira Tabassum** - Data Mining vs Data Science: The
Key Differences for Data Analysts - https://ca-
reerkarma.com/blog/data-mining-vs-data-science/

[11] HBR - Visualisations That Really Work. Link:
https://hbr.org/2016/06/visualisations-that-really-work

[12] **Oracle Exalytics** is a complete solution that includes best-
in-class hardware, an enterprise. Business Analytics platform and
In-Memory analytics software optimised to work together.

Rowley, Jennifer (2007). The wisdom hierarchy: representations of the DIKW hierarchy. Journal of Information and
Communication Science. 33 (2): 163–180.

Rowley, Jennifer; Richard Hartley (2006). Organising
knowledge: an introduction to managing access to information.

Yudono, Adipandang (2015). Hierarchy of Data-Information-Knowledge-Wisdom (DIKW) in understanding science's level to empirical phenomena from fact to theory. Retrieved 28 August 2017 http://www.kompasiana.com/

Zeleny, Milan (2005). Human systems management: integrating knowledge, management and systems. World Scientific.
15–16

Zins, Chaim (2007) - Conceptual approaches to defining
data, information, and knowledge. Journal of the American Society for Information Science and Technology. 58 (4): 479–493.

A Mathematical Theory of Communication by Claude
Shannon (1948)

Computing Machinery and Intelligence by Alan Turing
(1950)

A Business Intelligence System by Hans Peter Luhn (1958)

The Future of Data Analysis by John W. Tukey (1962)

Concise Survey of Computer Methods by Peter Naur (1974)

Exploratory Data Analysis by John W. Tukey (1977)

The Relational Model for Database Management by Edgar F. Codd (1990)

Data Science: An Action Plan for Expanding the Technical Areas of the Field of Statistics by William S. Cleveland

Long-lived Digital Data Collections: Enabling Research and Education in the 21st Century by The National Science Board

Statistical Modeling: The Two Cultures by Leo Breiman

MapReduce: simplified data processing on large clusters by Jeffrey Dean and Sanjay Ghemawat

Competing on Analytics by Thomas H. Davenport

Introduction to Dataology and Data Science by Yangyong Zhu and Yun Xiong

Data Scientist: The Sexiest Job of the 21st Century by Thomas H. Davenport and D.J. Patil

Digital Transformation (DX) means applying new technologies to radically change processes, customer experience, and value. DX allows organisations to become Digital Native Enterprise that support innovation and digital disruption rather than enhancing existing technologies and models.

Omnicanality: Integration of all channels through which customers communi-cate with a company and subsequent management to give a homogeneous message through all of them.

Marc Prensky (2001) first introduced the concepts of digital native and digital immigrant.

Eric Almquist (March 2018) - How Digital Natives Are Changing B2B Purchasing - https://hbr.org/2018/03/how-digital-natives-are-changing-b2b-purchasing

Jared Spataro, Corporate Vice President for Microsoft 365 (April 30, 2020) - https://www.microsoft.com/en-us/microsoft-365/blog/2020/04/30/2-years-digital-transformation-2-months/

International Data Centre (IDC) - FutureScape: Worldwide IT Industry 2019 Predictions - idc.com/getdoc.jsp?containerId=US44403818

Capgemini - Understanding Digital Mastery Today - https://www.capgemini.com/understanding-digital-mastery-today

The Enterprisers Project (A community helping CIOs and IT leaders solve problems) - What is digital transformation? - https://enterprisersproject.com/what-is-digital-transformation

Marc Saxer (12 May 2015) - Shaping The Great Digital Transformation. https://www.socialeurope.eu/shaping-great-digital-transformation

Ikhlaq Sidhu, (May 2020), - Covid-19 is the biggest driver of dig-ital transfor-mation yet" - https://timesofindia.indiatimes.com/blogs/voices/covid-19-is-the-biggest-driver-of-digital-transformation-yet/

Marc Benioff - "What Is Digital Transformation?", published in Salesforce web-site - https://www.salesforce.com/products/platform/what-is-digital-transformation/

Gartner - is a registered trademark and service mark of Gartner, Inc. and/or its affiliates in the U.S. and internationally, and all references about Gartner in this book are used herein with permission after their careful revisions.

Katrina Aaslaid (November 2018) - https://valuer.ai/blog/50-examples-of-corporations-that-failed-to-innovate-and-missed-their-chance/

Sylvain Saurel – (August 2019) 6 Reasons Why Yahoo! Failed - https://medium.com/swlh/6-reasons-why-yahoo-failed-6004d67e86ff

www.ingramcontent.com/pod-product-compliance
Lightning Source LLC
Chambersburg PA
CBHW031826170526
45157CB00001B/197